First World War
and Army of Occupation
War Diary
France, Belgium and Germany

62 DIVISION
Divisional Troops
Divisional Ammunition Column
12 January 1917 - 31 August 1919

WO95/3075/3

The Naval & Military Press Ltd
www.nmarchive.com
Published in association with The National Archives

Published by

The Naval & Military Press Ltd

Unit 10 Ridgewood Industrial Park,

Uckfield, East Sussex,

TN22 5QE England

Tel: +44 (0) 1825 749494

www.naval-military-press.com

www.nmarchive.com

This diary has been reprinted in facsimile from the original. Any imperfections are inevitably reproduced and the quality may fall short of modern type and cartographic standards.

© Crown Copyright
Images reproduced by permission of The National Archives, London, England, 2015.

Contents

Document type	Place/Title	Date From	Date To
Heading	WO95/3075-3		
Heading	62nd Division 62nd Divl Ammn Colmn Jan 1917 1919 Aug		
Heading	War Diary of 62nd Divisional Ammunition Column From 12.1.17 To 31.1.17 Volume I		
War Diary	Northampton	12/01/1917	15/01/1917
War Diary	Mezerolles	19/01/1917	20/01/1917
War Diary	Authieule	23/01/1917	23/01/1917
War Diary	Couin	24/01/1917	24/01/1917
War Diary	Thievres	24/01/1917	31/01/1917
Operation(al) Order(s)	62nd Divisional Ammn Col Operation Order No.3	20/01/1917	20/01/1917
Operation(al) Order(s)	62nd Divisional Artillery Operation Order No.1	19/01/1917	19/01/1917
Miscellaneous	March Table		
Operation(al) Order(s)	62 D.A.C Operation Order No.2	23/01/1917	23/01/1917
Operation(al) Order(s)	62nd Divisional Artillery Operation Order No.3	21/01/1917	21/01/1917
Miscellaneous	March Table 62nd Div Artillery		
Heading	War Diary 62nd Divisional Ammunition Column From 1st February 1917 To 28th February 1917 Volume II		
War Diary	Thievres	01/02/1917	04/02/1917
War Diary	P 2d 55	05/02/1917	28/02/1917
Heading	War Diary 62nd Divisional Ammunition Column From 1st March 1917 To 31st March 1917 Volume III		
War Diary	P 23d	01/03/1917	04/03/1917
War Diary	Hamel	05/03/1917	21/03/1917
War Diary	Miraumont	22/03/1917	31/03/1917
Heading	War Diary 62nd Divisional Ammunition Column From 1st April 1917 To 30th April 1917 Volume IV		
War Diary	Miraumont L.36.a	01/04/1917	11/04/1917
War Diary	G.4.d.6.8	12/04/1917	30/04/1917
Heading	War Diary 62nd Div Amm Column Volume V From 1st May 1917 To 31st May 1917		
War Diary	G.4.d.6.8	01/05/1917	31/05/1917
Heading	War Diary of 62nd Divisional Ammunition Column From 1st June 1917 To 30th June 1917 Volume VI		
War Diary	G.4.d.6.8	01/06/1917	22/06/1917
War Diary	H.22.b.0.5	23/06/1917	30/06/1917
Heading	War Diary of 62nd Divisional Ammunition Column From 1st July 1917 To 31st July 1917 Volume VII		
War Diary	H.22.b.0.5	01/07/1917	31/07/1917
Heading	War Diary of 62nd Divisional Ammunition Column From 1st August 1917 To 31st August 1917 Volume VIII		
War Diary	H.22.B.0.5	01/08/1917	31/08/1917
Heading	War Diary of 62nd Divisional Ammunition Column From 1st September 1917 To 30th September 1917 Volume IX		
War Diary	H.22.b.0.5	01/09/1917	30/09/1917
Heading	War Diary of 62nd Divisional Ammunition Column From 1st October 1917 To 31st October 1917 Volume X		

War Diary	H.22.b05	01/10/1917	26/10/1917
War Diary	S.7.b	27/10/1917	31/10/1917
Heading	War Diary of 62nd Divisional Ammunition Column From 1st November 1917 To 31st November 1917 Volume XI		
War Diary	S.7.b.3.3	01/11/1917	10/11/1917
War Diary	S.26.a.9.9	11/11/1917	17/11/1917
War Diary	N.5.C.1.8	18/11/1917	19/11/1917
War Diary	P.16.a. (57C)	20/11/1917	20/11/1917
War Diary	Q.19.6. (57c)	21/11/1917	23/11/1917
War Diary	(Map 57C) Q 19.b.4.3	24/11/1917	30/11/1917
Heading	War Diary of 62nd Divisional Ammunition Column From 1st December 1917 To 31st December 1917 Volume XII		
War Diary	(57C) Q19b.4.3	01/12/1917	02/12/1917
War Diary	P.22.d.4.7	02/12/1917	08/12/1917
War Diary	Q.2.4 Central	09/12/1917	16/12/1917
War Diary	1.27. Central	17/12/1917	28/12/1917
War Diary	G.14 Central	29/12/1917	29/12/1917
War Diary	Lens 11/100000	30/12/1917	31/12/1917
War Diary	Lens 11 1/40000 Gauchin Legal	01/01/1918	12/01/1918
War Diary	Gauchin Legal Lens 11.1/100000	13/01/1918	15/01/1918
War Diary	Anzin Ref Map 51.B. G.7.D.5.7	16/01/1918	26/01/1918
War Diary	G.2.D.5.7.51.B	27/01/1918	31/01/1918
Heading	War Diary of 62nd Div Amm Column From Feb 1st 1918 To Feb 28th 1918 Volume XIV		
War Diary	G.7.d. Sheet 51.b	01/02/1918	15/02/1918
War Diary	Lens 11/10000 Gauchin Legal	16/02/1918	28/02/1918
Heading	62nd Divisional Artillery War Diary 62nd Divisional Ammunition Column R.F.A. March 1918		
Heading	War Diary of 62nd Divisional Ammunition Column From 1st March 1918 To 31st March 1918 Volume VI		
War Diary	Lens II 1/10000 Gauchin Legal	01/03/1918	05/03/1918
War Diary	G.1.d.6.5.51b	06/03/1918	22/03/1918
War Diary	(51 B) G.13.d.	24/03/1918	24/03/1918
War Diary	(57 D) D.30.a.d.9	25/03/1918	26/03/1918
War Diary	(57d) D.15.d.93	27/03/1918	31/03/1918
Heading	62nd Divisional Artillery War Diary 62nd Divisional Ammunition Column R.F.A. April 1918		
Heading	War Diary of 62nd Div Amm Col From 1st April 1918 To 30th April 1918 Volume IV		
War Diary	Sheet 57d D.15.d 9.3	01/04/1918	01/04/1918
War Diary	J.2.c.5.5	02/04/1918	17/04/1918
War Diary	D.19.d.3.8	18/04/1918	30/04/1918
Heading	War Diary of 62nd Divisional Ammunition Column Volume XVII From 1st May 1918 To 31st May 1918		
War Diary	Sheet 57d 1/40,000 D.19.d.3.8	01/05/1918	03/05/1918
War Diary	I 11d.5.8	04/05/1918	31/05/1918
Heading	War Diary of 62nd Divisional Ammunition Column From 1st June 1918 To 30th June 1918 Volume VI		
War Diary	Sheet 57D 1/40,000 I IId.5.8	01/06/1918	26/06/1918
War Diary	Sheet 57D 1/40,000 Amplier	27/06/1918	30/06/1918
Heading	Divl Artillery 62nd Division 62nd Divisional Ammunition Column July 1918		
War Diary	Sheet 57D 1/40,000 Amplier	01/07/1918	16/07/1918
War Diary	50 Sheet 1/80,000 Challons	17/07/1918	19/07/1918

War Diary	Sheet 34 1/80,000 Reims	20/07/1918	31/07/1918
Heading	War Diary 62nd Divisional Trench Mortar Bties Volume XX From August 1st 1918 To August 31st 1918		
War Diary	Authie Cadran Cross Roads	01/08/1918	01/08/1918
War Diary	Plivot	02/08/1918	03/08/1918
War Diary	Authie	05/08/1918	20/08/1918
War Diary	Bucquoy	21/08/1918	26/08/1918
War Diary	Authie	31/08/1918	31/08/1918
Heading	War Diary of 62nd Divisional Ammunition Column From 1st September 1918 To 30th September 1918 Volume XXI		
War Diary	Ref Map 57c 1/40000 S.14.c.2.4	01/09/1918	14/09/1918
War Diary	Ref Map 57c 1/40000 I.27. Central	15/09/1918	30/09/1918
Heading	War Diary of 62nd Divisional Ammunition Column From 1st October 1918 To 31st October 1918 Volume XXII		
War Diary	57.b.1/40000	01/10/1918	31/10/1918
Heading	War Diary of 62nd Divisional Ammunition Column From 1st November 1918 To 31st November 1918 Volume XXIII		
War Diary	Map 57"B" 1/40000	01/11/1918	02/11/1918
War Diary	Map 51"A" 1/40000	03/11/1918	04/11/1918
War Diary	Map 51 1/40000	05/11/1918	18/11/1918
War Diary	Map Namur-8 1/100000	19/11/1918	30/11/1918
Heading	War Diary of 62nd Divisional Ammunition Column From 1st December 1918 To 31st December 1918 Volume XXIV		
War Diary	Map Namur 8 1/100000 Lisogne	01/12/1918	09/12/1918
War Diary	Map Marche 1/100000	10/12/1918	16/12/1918
War Diary	Map Germany 1/M 1/100000	17/12/1918	21/12/1918
War Diary	Map Germany 1/L 1/100000	22/12/1918	31/12/1918
War Diary	Call Germany	01/01/1919	31/01/1919
Heading	War Diary 62nd Divl Arty February 1919 Vol XIV		
War Diary	Call Germany	01/02/1919	28/02/1919
Heading	War Diary Original Highland Divisional Ammunition Column Volume No.27 March		
War Diary	Call Germany	01/03/1919	16/05/1919
War Diary	Burvenich	16/05/1919	31/05/1919
Heading	War Diary of D.A.C. Highland Division Form 1/6/19 To 30/6/19		
War Diary	Burvenich Germany	01/06/1919	30/06/1919
Heading	War Diary Highland Divisional Ammn Column July 1919 Volume No.7		
War Diary	Burvenich Germany	01/07/1919	31/07/1919
Heading	War Diary Highland Divisional Ammn Column August 1919 Volume No.8		
War Diary	Codford Wilts	01/08/1919	31/08/1919

W957/3076(1)

62ND DIVISION

62ND DIVL AMMN COLMN
JAN 1917-DEC 1918
1919 AUG

ORIGINAL

Vol 1

SECRET.

WAR DIARY.

of

62nd Divisional Ammunition Column

From 12.1.17 to 31.1.17.

VOLUME I.

Jan. 1917

WAR DIARY or **INTELLIGENCE SUMMARY**
(Erase heading not required.)

Army Form C. 2118.

62 D.A.C.

Place	Date	Hour	Summary of Events and Information	Remarks and references to Appendices
	Jan. 1917			
No.Hampton	12th		No 2 Section proceeded to Havre kei Southampton and Havre. After staying a night at Havre the Section went to Mezerolles. No difficulty was encountered during the move.	
Southampton	13th		No 3 Section moved to the same destination via Havre.	
Southampton	14th		No 4 Section moved to the same destination via Havre. No 1	
Southampton	15th		HQ's and No 1 Section moved abroad HQrs to Mezerolles. No 1 Section to Rohan-le-haud. Although there was 3 accident during the move Invisible.	
Mezerolles	19th		Had the men did well. Orders were received to rearrange the D.A.C. "A" Echelon became 6 Sections - whilst a proportion of "B" was handed to the 311 Army F.ld Brigade A.C.	
MEZEROLLES etc			Received orders to march on 23rd Jan - issued mark orders to "A" third-attached "A"	"A"

J. Witcher Lieut
(command 62 D.O.C)

Army Form C. 2118.

62 D.A.C

WAR DIARY
or
INTELLIGENCE SUMMARY
(Erase heading not required.)

Place	Date	Hour	Summary of Events and Information	Remarks and references to Appendices
AUTHEULE	23	8pm	Arrived at AUTHEULE - billets bad	
COUIN	24	8pm	A Schelon arrived at COUIN - men in tents - ther monastic down to 2°F - very little Sickness	
THIEVRES	24	8pm	B Schelon HQ staff + 311 Farr 3de B.A.C. arrived at THIEVRES men in billets	
THIEVRES	25	8pm	Ther monseter down to zero again but hardly any Sickness. Co. Visited A Schelon & HQ R.A at BUS les ARTOIS - men Schelon	
THIEVRES	26	8pm	Doing fatigues for the Div siar - more Schelon	
THIEVRES	27	8pm	" do " "	
THIEVRES	28	8pm	" do " "	
THIEVRES	29	8pm	" do " "	
THIEVRES	30	8pm	" do " "	
THIEVRES	31	8pm	Weather has been extremely trying and the men have only had our issue of blankets - 17 days - Supplies are more regular - Fuel very scarce J Mitchell (Lieut) RHA	

SECRET.

540/125/M.
Copy No. 5

62ND DIVISIONAL AMM. COL.

Operation Order No 1.

Reference Div.Art.Operation Order No 1 attached.

Sections will move off at the following times.

H.Q. and A. Echelon	12-7 pm
B.A.C.511 A.A.Bde	11-32 am
B. Echelon	11-20 pm

R. M.

Lieut-Col.,
Comdg 62 D.A.C.

20.1.1917.

Copy No 1. No 1 Sect. late No 3.
" No 2 No 2 Sect. late No 2.
" No 3 No 511 Army Art Bde Amm.Col.
" No 4 No 4 Section.
" No 5)
" No 6) War Diary.

DAC/126/M.   Copy No....

SECRET.

62nd Divisional Artillery.
Operation Order No 1.

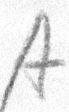

Reference Map 1/100,000 LENS Sheet 11.

1. The 62nd Divnl Artillery and 525 Co.ASC will move through XIII Corps Area into the V Corps Area on 23rd and 24th January.

2. March table for January 23rd attached.

3. 500 yards interval will be maintained between each Artillery Brigade and between Brigades and D.A.C. 200 yards interval will be kept between batteries and sections of D.A.C.

4. Attention is directed to Divnl War Standing Orders Sect.2.

5. Supply Refilling point for 22nd January on FROHEN- LE-GRAND- MEZEROLLES Road as at present at 3 pm.

6. Baggage wagons of Artillery Units will be loaded on the morning of the 23rd January and will rejoin the baggage section of the train by 9-30 am.

7. The Supply Section of the Train will march under the orders of O.C.Train.

8. Billeting parties of units will report to Staff Captain R.A. at AUTHIEULE Church at 2.30 pm on 22nd January.

9. Divisional Artillery Headquarters will close at WAVANS at 9 am on 23rd and re-open at AMPLIER at the same hour.

sd W.G.Lindsell
Capt RA
Brigade Major 62nd Div.Arty.

19.1.1917.

MARCH TABLE.
62nd Div. Arty.

Date.	Units in order of march	Starting Point	Time.	Route	Destination.
23rd Jan.	312 Bde RFA	Cross Rds OCCOCHES	11-30am	MEZEROLLES - DOULLENS ROAD	The area between DOULLENS (inclusive) and ORVILLE inclusive on both roads between DOULLENS and ORVILLE
" "	311 Bde RFA	do.	11-57am		
" "	H.Q. 62 Div. Art	do.	12.17pm		
" "	310 Bde RFA	do.	12.20pm		
" "	H.Q. and A. Ech. D.A.C.	do.	12.47pm		
" "	B.A.C. of 311 A.A.Bde	do.	1.15pm		
" "	B. Echelon D.A.C	do.	1.20 pm		
" "	525 Co. ASC baggage sect.	do.	1.35pm		

Remarks :-   Representative of Unit billeting parties will meet their units at the Road and Railway Crossing WEST END of DOULLENS and guide them to billets.

No Units will enter DOULLENS before 12 noon.

Guides for supply and baggage wagons will meet their wagons at AUTHIEULE.

D.A.C. wagons will not pull out on to the road in present area until 310 Bde RFA has passed.

Copy No. 5

SECRET

62 DAC Operation Order No 2

Reference map
1/40,000 Sheet 57D.
reference to Operation order as attached.

1. A. Echelon under Capt. Fraser will march at 9.55 am

2. H.Q. DAC, BAC 311 A.A.B. will march at 10-17 am

3. B. Echelon will march at 10-25 am.

23.1.17

Checked Lt & Adjt
62 DAC

Copy No. 1 311 AA BAC   Copy No. 5)
 "   "   2. Mov. Sect   "   6) War diary
 "   "   3. No 2
 "   "   4. B Echelon

62nd Divisional Artillery.

Operation Order No 2.

Reference Map
1/40,000 Sheet 57.D.   21st Jan. 1917.

1. The 62nd Divisional Artillery and 525 Co. A.S.C. will continue its march on 24th January from XIth Corps area to Vth Corps area in accordance with attached march table.

2. Intervals between units will be maintained as ordered for march of 23rd January.

3. Supply refilling point on 23rd January on DOULLENS - BOUQUEMAISON Road South of Rte VISEE (reference 1/100,000 LENS.II) at 2.30 pm.
   Supply refilling point on 24th January on ARQUEVES - ?? Road hour to be notified later, 12 noon.

4. Baggage wagons of units will be billeted with their Units on night 23/24 and will march with them on 24th January, rejoining 525 Co. A.S.C. in the BOIS-DU-WARNIMONT on morning of 25th January.

5. Billeting parties of Units will proceed their Units on the morning of 24th January reporting to the DO R Majors in their respective new areas not later than 10 am.

6. Divisional Artillery Headquarters will remain at AMPLIER on 24th January and March on 25th January to BUS-LES-ARTOIS.

            sd J. Anhoeld Capt DA
        Brigade Major RA 62nd Division.

MARCH TABLE 62nd Div ARTILLERY

DATE	UNITS IN ORDER OF MARCH	STARTING POINT	TIME	ROUTE	DESTINATION	REMARKS
11th Jan	311 Bde RFA		9.45am	SARTON MARIEUX LOUVENCOURT	ACHEUX WOOD	AND CAMP P24.77
"	312 Bde RFA	CROSS ROADS SOUTH OF ORVILLE H.10.c.8.2	10.15am	SARTON MARIEUX	LOUVENCOURT	
"	310 Bde RFA		10.45am	—do—	LOUVENCOURT	P24 VAUCHELLES
"	A ECHELON DAC		11.5am	SARTON AUTHIE	COURN	
"	Hq DAC BAC 311 HA Bde		11.27am	SARTON	THIEVRES	
"	B ECHELON DAC		11.35am	SARTON	THIEVRES	
"	525 Co ASC		11.50am	SARTON AUTHIE	BOIS DU WARNIMONT	

Original
Vol 2

War Diary

62nd Divisional Ammunition Column.

Volume II

From 1st February 1917
To 28th February 1917

62 D.A.C

Army Form C. 2118.

WAR DIARY
or
INTELLIGENCE SUMMARY.
(Erase heading not required.)

Instructions regarding War Diaries and Intelligence Summaries are contained in F.S. Regs., Part II. and the Staff Manual respectively. Title pages will be prepared in manuscript.

Place	Date	Hour	Summary of Events and Information	Remarks and references to Appendices
THIEVRES	1/2/17	8pm	Nothing of importance — weather very cold	
"	2/2/17	8pm	"	
"	3/2/17	8pm	"	
"	4/2/17	8pm	"	
P2 D.5.5"	5/2/17	8pm	Moved into the line — took over from 7 Bde.	
"	6/2/17	6pm	Reccn. the supply of gun ammunition to 14K, 22W & 35K N Bde	
"	7/2/17	6pm	continuing supply.	
"	8/2/17	6pm	"	
"	9/2/17	6pm	"	
"	10/2/17	6pm	"	
"	11/2/17	8pm	all horses inspected by C.O. personally in the H.O.I/c	
"	12.2.17	8pm	with special reference to mange outbreak.	
"	13.2.17	8pm	"	
"	14/2/17	8pm	Took over forward parade dump from 32. Bde. P.17.a.5.2	
"	15.2.17		inspected F.G. Dumps — thaw started.	

J Wadsworth MajGen
Commanding

WAR DIARY
or
INTELLIGENCE SUMMARY.
(Erase heading not required.)

Army Form C. 2118.

62 D.A.C.

Place	Date	Hour	Summary of Events and Information	Remarks and references to Appendices
P2 D55	16th	8pm	Took over A.B.C.D. dumps from 32 DAC. Posted 1 Officer and 40 O.R. with B wagons at "A".	
P2 D55	17th	8pm	Continuing supply of ammunition.	
"	18th	8pm	"	
"	19th	8pm	"	
"	20th	8pm	" Increased staff at D Dump	
"	21st	8pm	"	
"	22	8pm	"	
"	23	8pm	Handed over "A" Dump to 11th D.A.C.	
"	24	8pm	Warned to be in readiness to send 80 mules for pack transport work.	
"	25	8pm	Sent 184 mules to MAILLY to assist infantry - all ammunition wagons in "A" echelon filled	
"	26	8pm	Nothing of importance. Demand small.	
"	27	8pm	Received orders to move forward 1 section to carry ammunition up to pack animals	
"	28	8pm	No 2 Section moved to HAMEL.	

J. Mitchell Mel
Lieut Col
Commanding 62 DAC

Original

Vol 3

War Diary

62nd Divisional Ammunition Column.

Volume III

From 1st March 1917
To 31st March 1917.

ORIGINAL
62 D.A.

MARCH 1917

Army Form C. 2118.

WAR DIARY
or
INTELLIGENCE SUMMARY
(Erase heading not required.)

Place	Date	Hour	Summary of Events and Information	Remarks and references to Appendices
D23d	1st	8pm	Supplying ammunition	
"	2	8pm	"	
"	3	8pm	Formed pack section at HAMEL	
"	4	8pm	Pack section working	
HAMEL	5	8pm	Moved remainder A Echelon with 311 to HAMEL	lost 1 man killed 2 wounded 3rd
"	6	8pm	10 H.V. shells hit A166 camp - damage nil	
"	7	8pm	Bitterly cold wind	
"	8	8pm	5 H.V. shells fell nr camp. Damage nil - ammunition arrangements changed	
"	9	8pm	Nothing of importance	
"	10	8pm	Ordered to dump ammunition at MILL ROAD - HAMEL	
"	11	8pm	Nothing of importance	
"	12	8pm	Supply ammunition up to batteries	
"	13	8pm	"	
"	14	8pm	"	
"	15	8pm	"	
"	16	8pm	Very wet - traffic conditions bad	

J. Hutchings
Commander 62

ORIGINAL
62 S.A.L.

MARCH 1917

WAR DIARY or INTELLIGENCE SUMMARY.
(Erase heading not required.)

Army Form C. 2118.

Place	Date	Hour	Summary of Events and Information	Remarks and references to Appendices
HAMEL	17th	8h.	Continuing supply	
"	18th	8h.	Moved 2 dumps forward	
"	19	8h.	Moved 1 dump to MIRAUMONT	
"	20	8h.	Employed collecting ammunition from battery positions	
"	21	9h.	"	
H.Q. MIRAUMONT	22	8h.	Moved to MIRAUMONT	
"	23	8h.	Hard frost - clearing backward Dumps into red	
"	24	8h.	"	
"	25	8h.	"	
"	26	8h.	Started forward Dump at BEHAGNIES	
"	27	8h.	Still collecting from backward Dumps	
"	28	8h.	"	
"	29	8h.	A.º1 Section moved to ACHIET le GRAND - weather bad -	
"	30	8h.	Lt COL MITCHELL proceeded on leave, temporary command during	
			on CAPT C.S WALKER	
"	31	6pm	Supplies of ammunition and Stores ammunition.	

C.S. Heston. Capt.
Cmd. 62nd D.A.C.

T.2134. Wt. W708—776. 500000. 4/16. Sir J. C. & S.

Secret

Vol 4

Original

War Diary

62ⁿᵈ Divisional Ammunition Column

Volume IV

From 1ˢᵗ April 1917
To 30ᵗʰ April 1917

ORIGINAL
APRIL 1917.   62 D.A.C.

Army Form C. 2118.

WAR DIARY
or
INTELLIGENCE SUMMARY.
(Erase heading not required.)

Place	Date	Hour	Summary of Events and Information	Remarks and references to Appendices
MIRAUMONT L.36.a	1/4/17	8/30 M	Supplying ammunition and salvage work for MIRAUMONT dump.	
"	2/4/17	"	ditto.	
"	3/4/17	"	ditto. 2/Lt. F.C. GREENWOOD evacuated sick.	
"	4/4/17	"	Supplying ammunition and salvage work.	
"	5/4/17	"	ditto	
"	6/4/17	"	Supplying ammunition. Salvage work practically ceased owing to supply of ammunition being exerted by H.Q.R.P. to have preference over all other work.	
"	"	"	No. 2 Section moved at short notice to ACHIET-LE-GRAND.	
"	7/4/17	"	No Supply or Salvage work. Lent for Q'Master work to 310 R.F.A and 312 R.F.A and 313 R.F.A	
"	"	"	50 drivers each + animals to No.1 Belgian Ambulance on Bridges & supply ammunition independently.	
"	8/4/17		Supply ammunition. 2/Lt. E.S.N. WILLIAMS proceeded sick.	
"	9/4/17		ditto	
"	10/4/17		H.Q.D.A.C moved to ACHIET-LE-GRAND. Guns G.S. Wagons recovered to meet "B" ECHELON. M.T. pro tem; ammunition Parkhorses to Section + Batteries	
"	11/4/17		"B" ECHELON moved to ACHIET-LE-GRAND. "A" ECHELON moved to A.H.L.S.S.	

C. Glazebrook
Col. 62 DAC.

ORIGINAL
APRIL 1917

62 D.A.C.

Army Form C. 2118.

WAR DIARY
INTELLIGENCE SUMMARY.
(Erase heading not required.)

Instructions regarding War Diaries and Intelligence Summaries are contained in F.S. Regs., Part II. and the Staff Manual respectively. Title pages will be prepared in manuscript.

Place	Date	Hour	Summary of Events and Information	Remarks and references to Appendices
G4 d 5.5	12/4/17	8 p.m.	Move secret near ACHIET-LE-GRAND Station. Loads on arrival of Guns. Relief of H.A.C. Guns.	
	13/4/17	"	Supply of ammunition continues	
	14/4/17	"	Lt. N. RICHARDSON A/a 62nd D.A.C. to join 192 Division as Acting Major BIGG, R.F.A. (who has been temporarily relieved) also O.C. advanced Battery of Ammunition.	
	15/4/17		CAPTAIN F.A. WOODCOCK R.F.A. assumed command of 62nd D.A.C. (vice 55th A.F.A. Bde.), temporary Command handed over to him by CAPTAIN C.S. WARNER.	
	16.4.17	8 am	Ammunition supply continued	
	17.4.17	"	" " "	
	18.4.17	"	" " "	
	19.4.17	"	" " "	Recommended N° 796450 Sgt W. Halter D.A.p.M.Ketd
	20.4.17	"	Ammunition supply continued	
	21.4.17	"	Army Commander. Genl Gough inspected A Echelon	
	22.4.17	"	Ammunition supply continued	
	23.4.17	"	" " "	
	24.4.17	"	Established forward Dump at Abbaye Mory "B" H.Q. S.A. Ricarts in Charge	
	25.4.17	"	Ammunition supply continued	Gwathorke Lieut Comdg 62 D.A.C.

ORIGINAL
APRIL 1917
62 D.A.C.

Army Form C. 2118.

WAR DIARY
or
INTELLIGENCE SUMMARY.
(Erase heading not required.)

Instructions regarding War Diaries and Intelligence Summaries are contained in F. S. Regs., Part II. and the Staff Manual respectively. Title pages will be prepared in manuscript.

Place	Date	Hour	Summary of Events and Information	Remarks and references to Appendices
G.4.d.6.8.	26.4.17	8 p.m	Ammunition supply continued	
"	27.4.17	"	" " "	
"	28.4.17	"	" " " N° 796450 Sjt. W. Hallen R.F.A. awarded the M. Medal	
"	29.4.17	"	" " "	
"	30.4.17	"	" " " G.O.C. 62nd Div inspected A. Echelon	
			Falconbocb trené 60	
			mony 62nd D.A.C.	

Original.

Vol 5

War Diary

62nd. Div. Amm. Column.

Volume V

From 1st May 1917
To 31st May 1917.

MAY 1917

62nd DAC

WAR DIARY
or
INTELLIGENCE SUMMARY
(Erase heading not required.)

Army Form C. 2118.

Instructions regarding War Diaries and Intelligence Summaries are contained in F. S. Regs., Part II. and the Staff Manual respectively. Title pages will be prepared in manuscript.

Place	Date	Hour	Summary of Events and Information	Remarks and references to Appendices
64D88	1-5-17	8pm	Supplying Ammunition	
"	2-5-17	"	"	
"	3-5-17	"	Sent 88 Mules on park work with Infantry	
"	4-5-17	"	"	
"	5-5-17	"	"	
"	6-5-17	"	Lieut R.S. Jones posted to 310 Brigade R.F.A.	
			2/Lieut J.E. Edmondson takes over Div Grenade Dump	
"	7-5-17	"	Lieut H. Spence joins from 310 Brigade R.F.A.	
"	8-5-17	"	2/Lieut A.E. Major arrived, posted to No.2 Section D.A.C.	
"	9-5-17	"	Supplying Ammunition	
"	10-5-17	"	"	
"	11-5-17	"	"	
"	12-5-17	"	Maj Nicholson leave for England	
"	12-5-17	"	1 Man killed 1 wounded at Horry Dump by shell fire	
"	13-5-17	"	Cricifix Dump closed	
			Supplying Ammunition	

[signature]
Lieut. Col. R.F.A.
Commanding 62nd Divisional Ammunition Column, R.F.A.

MAY 1917.

Army Form C. 2118.

62nd D.A.C.

WAR DIARY
or
INTELLIGENCE SUMMARY.
(Erase heading not required.)

Instructions regarding War Diaries and Intelligence Summaries are contained in F. S. Regs., Part II. and the Staff Manual respectively. Title pages will be prepared in manuscript.

Place	Date	Hour	Summary of Events and Information	Remarks and references to Appendices
G4 d 68	14.5.17	8 p.m.	Supplying Ammunition	
"	15.5.17	"	" Adjutant proceeds to England on leave	
"	16.5.17	"	"	
"	17.5.17	"	" Hony Bung Clerk Crucifix Dump, reopened Lieut H Spence admitted to Hospital	
"	18.5.17	"	"	
"	19.5.17	"	" B. Echelon moved to B.26-A.0.9. Capt Walker appointed O.C. Dumps	
"	20.5.17	"	" 2/Lt A. Wilson admitted to Hospital	
"	21.5.17	"	"	
"	22.5.17	"	"	
"	23.5.17	"	"	
"	24.5.17	"	" 2/Lt Owen. H.A. goes on leave	
"	25.5.17	"	" H.V. Gun shelled vicinity of camp /Area G.6/ early this morning	
"	25.5.17	"	Hostile aircraft flew over Camp about 10.45 p.m. dropped several bombs	
"	26.5.17	"	Supplying Ammunition. Serg. Calibre fire fired 19 rounds near Pashenay S.T. Many Errors	
"	27.5.17	"	" 2/Lt Rissole goes on leave	
"	28.5.17	"	" " Lieut Walker relieved	

Lieut: Col. R.F.A.
Commanding 62nd Divisional Ammunition Column C.F.A.

MAY 1917

62 DAC Army Form C. 2118.

WAR DIARY
or
INTELLIGENCE SUMMARY.
(Erase heading not required.)

Place	Date	Hour	Summary of Events and Information	Remarks and references to Appendices
G.4.d.68	29.5.17	8 p.m.	Handed over to 58 D.A.C. Horse, Tumbrins & Crucifix Dumps	
"	29.5.17		Moved B. Echelon & F.M. Batteries to area H.13 Central (approx)	
"	30.5.17		Very little doing	
"	31.5.17		Salvinging Ammunition	

Guezenloh
Lieut: Col. R.F.A.
Commanding 62nd Divisional Ammunition Column R.F.A.

Original

Vol 6

War Diary

of

62nd Divisional Ammunition Column

Volume VI

"From 1st June 1917
To 30th June 1917

JUNE 1917 — 62nd DAC

ORIGINAL WAR DIARY
INTELLIGENCE SUMMARY

Army Form C. 2118.

Place	Date	Hour	Summary of Events and Information	Remarks and references to Appendices
Eq d 6.8	1/6/17	6pm	Supplying Ammunition/Hold & Woolcott on leave	
"	2.6.17	6pm	Supplying Ammunition	
"	3.6.17	6pm	"	
"	4.6.17	6pm	"	
"	5.6.17	6pm	"	Captain T. Kirkby on leave.
"	6.6.17	6pm	"	
"	7.6.17	6pm	"	Lieutenant H. Smith on leave
"	8.6.17	6pm	"	Lieutenant L. Wilson " "
"	9.6.17	6pm	"	
"	10.6.17	6pm	"	Lieutenant G.R. Bottomley " "
"	11.6.17	6pm	"	
"	12.6.17	6pm	"	
"	13.6.17	8pm	"	52 Runners to posted to No. 3 Section.
"	14.6.17	8pm	"	
"	15.6.17	8pm	"	
"	16.6.17	8pm	"	

J. Fraser Capt. RFA

WAR DIARY

JUNE 1917 — ORIGINAL — 62nd D.A.C.

INTELLIGENCE SUMMARY.
Army Form C. 2118.

(Erase heading not required.)

Instructions regarding War Diaries and Intelligence Summaries are contained in F. S. Regs., Part II. and the Staff Manual respectively. Title pages will be prepared in manuscript.

Place	Date	Hour	Summary of Events and Information	Remarks and references to Appendices
Q.4.d.6.6.	17/6/17	8 a.m.	Supplying Ammunition	
"	18/6/17	"	"	
"	19/6/17	"	"	
"	20/6/17	"	"	
"	21/6/17	"	"	
"	22/6/17	"	Received instructions to move into 37th Div. Area	
"	23/6/17	"	Took over Vieux Jeury	
H.17.d.0.5.	24/6/17	"	Relieved 37th D.A.C.	
"	25/6/17	"	"	
"	26/6/17	"	{ 2/Lt J. Kennett joined & posted to No. 3 Section	
"	26/6/17	"	{ Div. Rearward Dump established at Beugnatre	
"	27/6/17	"	"	
"	28/6/17	"	"	
"	29/6/17	"	"	
"	30/6/17	"	"	

Greathed Lt Col
(commanding 62 D.A.C.)

Secret

Original

Confidential War Diary

of

62nd Divisional Ammunition Column

Volume VII

From 1st July 1917
To 31st July 1917

JULY 1917 ORIGINAL

62ND D.A.C.

Army Form C. 2118.

WAR DIARY
INTELLIGENCE SUMMARY
(Erase heading not required.)

Instructions regarding War Diaries and Intelligence Summaries are contained in F. S. Regs., Part II. and the Staff Manual respectively. Title pages will be prepared in manuscript.

Place	Date	Hour	Summary of Events and Information	Remarks and references to Appendices
H22 & O5	1st	8am	Supplying ammunition, horse fatigues & salving	
	2		" " " " " "	
	3		" " " 1 O.R. wounded	
	4		" " horse fatigues	
	5		" " salving	
	6		Supplying ammunition " 128 Remounts arrived (No 3 Section)	
	7		" " "	
	8		" " Inspection by G.O.C. 62 Div.	
	9		" " fatigues	
	10		" " salving	
	11		Supplying ammunition salving	
	12		" " "	
	13		" " " 96 Remounts (No 3 Section)	
	14		" " "	
	15		Supplying ammunition	
	16		" "	Two

July 1917 ORIGINAL

62nd D.A.C. Army Form C. 2118.

WAR DIARY

INTELLIGENCE SUMMARY.
(Erase heading not required.)

Place	Date	Hour	Summary of Events and Information	Remarks and references to Appendices
H.22.b.05	17	8p	Supplying Ammunition	
	18"	"	"	
	19	"	Lieut R. Walker posted to 310 Brigade	
	20	"	Inspection by G.O.C. R.A. VI Corps	
	21	"	" 2nd Lieut Capt C.S. Walker attached to 312 Brigade RFA	
	22	"	Supplying Ammunition	
	23	"	"	
	24	"	"	
	25	"	"	Nieuport-lez-
	26	"	Reinforcements joined and posted No 3 Section	
	27	"	Building winter quarters.	
	28	"	Salving Ammunition in forward area	
	29	"	Church Service conducted by Archbishop of York.	
	30	"	"	
	31	"	Inspection by Corps Commander.	
			J. Law Capt. RFA	

Original

Secret

Vol

War Diary

of

62nd Divisional Ammunition Column

Volume VIII

From 1st August 1917
To 31st August 1917.

August 1917

62nd D.A.C.

Army Form C. 2118.

WAR DIARY
~~INTELLIGENCE~~ SUMMARY
(Erase heading not required.)

ORIGINAL

Instructions regarding War Diaries and Intelligence Summaries are contained in F. S. Regs., Part II. and the Staff Manual respectively. Title pages will be prepared in manuscript.

Place	Date	Hour	Summary of Events and Information	Remarks and references to Appendices
H. 22. B.0.5.	1-8-17	8pm	Supplying Ammunition Salving S.A.A.	
	2.8.17		" " General Salvage	
	3.8.17		" "	
	4.8.17		" " General Salvage	
	5.8.17		Church Parade (3rd Anniversary of entry into the War) General Salvage	
	6.8.17		Work under Lieut. Joyce Symons	
	7.8.17		" " Salvage	
	8.8.17		" "	
	9.8.17			
	10.8.17		Colonel J.W. Woodroe returned from Leie leave and re-assumes Command.	
	11.8.17		Supplying Ammunition 10-8-1917. J. Laser Capt. R.F.A. General Salvage	
	12.8.17		" "	
	13.8.17		" "	

Army Form C. 2118.

WAR DIARY
or
INTELLIGENCE SUMMARY.
(Erase heading not required.)

Instructions regarding War Diaries and Intelligence Summaries are contained in F. S. Regs., Part II. and the Staff Manual respectively. Title pages ORIGINAL will be prepared in manuscript.

Place	Date	Hour	Summary of Events and Information	Remarks and references to Appendices
R.22.B.0.5	14.8.17	8.17 8 p.m.	Supplying Ammunition - General Salvage	
"	15.8.17		"	
"	16.8.17		Received instructions to reorganize establishment of D.A.C. No. 3 Section becoming L.A.A. Section	
"	17.8.17		Supplying Ammunition. New Establishment D.A.C. Completed.	
"	18.8.17		General Salvage	
"	19.8.17		"	
"	20.8.17		"	
"	21.8.17		"	
"	22.8.17		Supplying Ammunition. General Salvage. G.O.C.R.A. inspected Column in F.S.M. Order.	
"	23.8.17		Supplying Ammunition. General Salvage. 70 L.D. Animals handed over to 58th Div Artillery, surplus to new Establishment	
"	24.8.17		Supplying Ammunition. General Salvage.	
"	25.8.17		"	
"	26.8.17		"	

WAR DIARY
or
INTELLIGENCE SUMMARY.

Army Form C. 2118.

Place	Date	Hour	Summary of Events and Information	Remarks and references to Appendices
H.29.B.0.5.	27.8.17	8/178 p.m.	Supplying Ammunition & General Salvage. 2 N.C.O.s & 15 Drivers posted to 310 Brigade R.F.A. Surplus to new Establishment	
	28.8.17		Supplying Ammunition & General Salvage. 38 Mules 18. G.S. wagons sent / Maltese Cart despatched to Advanced Horse Transport Depot ABBEVILLE, Surplus to new Establishment	
	29.8.17		Supplying Ammunition & General Salvage.	
	30.8.17		" " " "	
	31.8.17		" " " "	

J. Allcock Lieut. Col.
Commdg. 62. D.A.C.

Original

War Diary

of

62nd Divisional Ammunition Column

Volume IX

From 1st September 1917
To 30th September 1917

SEPTEMBER 1917.

62nd D.A.C.

Army Form C. 2118.

WAR DIARY
INTELLIGENCE SUMMARY.

ORIGINAL

(Erase heading not required.)

Place	Date	Hour	Summary of Events and Information	Remarks and references to Appendices
H35.d.0.5	1st	8pm	Ammunition Gun Supply & General Salvage.	
	2nd		" " "	
	3rd		1 B.C, 1 S.S & 11 Drivers transferred to 310 & 312 Brigade.	
	4th		Ammunition Supply & General Salvage	
	5th		" " "	
	6th		" " 3.O.R. wounded.	
	7th		" " "	
	8th		Ammunition Supply & General Salvage.	
	9th		" " "	
	10th		" " "	
	11th		" " "	
	12th		Ammunition Supply & General Salvage. 1 O.R. wounded	
	13th		" " "	Gunner of ___ Regt
	14th		" " "	joined 62 D.A.C
	15th		" " "	
	16th		" " " 1 O.R transferred to 62 T.M.Bn	

SEPTEMBER 1917

62ND D.A.C.

Army Form C. 2118.

WAR DIARY
~~INTELLIGENCE SUMMARY~~ ORIGINAL
(Erase heading not required.)

Instructions regarding War Diaries and Intelligence Summaries are contained in F.S. Regs., Part II. and the Staff Manual respectively. Title pages will be prepared in manuscript.

Place	Date	Hour	Summary of Events and Information	Remarks and references to Appendices
H22 d5	17th	8 p.m.	Ammunition Supply & General Salvage	
	18th	"	" Lieut G.R. Bottomley posted to 62 Y Halve	
	19th	"	" Transferred 8 Gunners & 9 Drivers to 62 Y Finton	
	20th	"	Ammunition Supply & General Salvage. Inspected No 1 & 2 Section	
	21st	"	" "	
	22	"	" "	
	23	"	" " Inspected No 3 Section	
	24	"	Ammunition Supply & General Salvage	
	25	"	" "	
	26	"	" "	
	27	"	Ammunition Supply & General Salvage	
	28	"	" "	Groenenberg 61 D.S.A.
	29	"	" "	Lt T.B. Willis Joined from (?)
	30	"	" "	J. Laws Capt RGA T. Cmdg 62 D.A.C.

Original

Secret

Vol 10

War Diary

of

62nd Divisional Ammunition Column

Volume X

From 1st October 1917
To 31st October 1917

OCTOBER 1917. ORIGINAL

62nd D.A.C.

Army Form C. 2118.

WAR DIARY

INTELLIGENCE SUMMARY.

(Erase heading not required.)

Instructions regarding War Diaries and Intelligence
Summaries are contained in F. S. Regs., Part II.
and the Staff Manual respectively. Title pages
will be prepared in manuscript.

Place	Date	Hour	Summary of Events and Information	Remarks and references to Appendices
H.22.b.05	1 x 17	9 am	Supply of Ammunition & Salvage.	
	2 x 17		" "	
	3 x 17		" "	
	4 x 17		" "	
	5 x 17		" "	
	6 x 17		" Summer time ceases tonight. Write time. Clock back 1 hour.	
	7 x 17		" "	
	8 x 17		" "	
	9 x 17		" "	
	10 x 17		" 2/Lt. F. Woodcock having reported from leave resumes command.	

J. Fraser Capt RFA

OCTOBER 1917

ORIGINAL WAR DIARY
INTELLIGENCE SUMMARY
(Erase heading not required.)

Army Form C. 2118.

62 DAC

Place	Date	Hour	Summary of Events and Information	Remarks and references to Appendices
HZBOS	11th		Ammunition Supply and General Salvage	Capt V.H. Story admitted to Hospital
	12		" " " "	Lieut A Wilson appointed Actg Asst
	13		" " " "	
	14		" " " "	
	15		Ammunition Supply	
	16		" "	
	17		" "	
	18		" "	Todo recd 71 Remount for 3rd Div Artillery
	19		Ammunition Supply & General Salvage	
	20		" " " "	C.R.A 3rd Div Coly inspected Camps
	21		" " " "	
	22		" " " "	
	23		Ammunition Supply & General Salvage	
	24		" " " "	3rd Div Arty took over 70 Remounts
	25		" " " "	
	26		" " " "	Available Supplies to move to new Camps Col.

Lieut Col
62 D.A.C.

OCTOBER 1917   ORIGINAL   62 D.A.C.   Army Form C. 2118.

WAR DIARY
INTELLIGENCE SUMMARY.
(Erase heading not required.)

Place	Date	Hour	Summary of Events and Information	Remarks and references to Appendices
H.Q.6 as S.7.b	26th	8p.m	Handed over throught Stores to 3rd Div. Amm. Column. Took over No. 11 A.R.P.	
	27		Handed over Camps to 3rd D.A.C. Column moved to new area in S.7.b (51B)	
	28		Ammunition Supply	
	29		" "	
	30		" "	
	31		" Capt. V.H.S. Long. Adjutant returns from Hospital	

H Crockford Lt 62 DAC
62. D.A.C.

Original

Vol II

War Diary
of
62ⁿᵈ Divisional Ammunition Column

Volume XI

From 1ˢᵗ November 1917
To 31ˢᵗ November 1917

WAR DIARY

INTELLIGENCE SUMMARY

NOVEMBER 1917

62 D.A.C.

Army Form C. 2118.

Place	Date	Hour	Summary of Events and Information	Remarks and references to Appendices
S.7 & 33.	1	8 pm	Ammunition Supply & Salvage.	
	2	"	"	
	3	"	"	
	4	"	Ammunition Supply & Salvage.	
	5	"	"	
	6	"	"	
	7	"	"	
	8	"	"	
	9	"	Ammunition Supply & Salvage.	
	10	"	"	
S.26 d 9	11	"	Ammunition Supply. Moved to Area L.28.a (51.B) Handed over Hostels to 310 Brigade and 19.b. 812 Brigade. Handed Vacated Camps over to 34 & D.A.C.	
	12	"	Ammunition Supply. Handed over 11 A.R.P. to 34 Div Artillery	
	13	"	Ammunition Supply. Lieut F. Kennett + 18 O.R (N.C.O & Army Personnel)	
	13	"	P.G.A.9.1 (57c) on embarkation for 62 Div Q.	

Yslearworth Lieut Col 62 D.A.C.
Commdg 62. D.A.C.

NOVEMBER 1917
62) D.A.C.
ORIGINAL
Army Form C. 2118.

WAR DIARY
or
INTELLIGENCE SUMMARY.
(Erase heading not required.)

Place	Date	Hour	Summary of Events and Information	Remarks and references to Appendices
S26a99d4th		8am	Assisting Infantry Brigade to move. Clearing up camp vacated by Brigade. Silvery motored left to Aerodrome Camp. Capt V.H.S Long. Adjutant admitted to Hospital. Lieut A. Leake appointed Acting Adjutant	
"	15		Clearing up camps & taking over	
"	16		" " " & Remount nurses	
"	17		Moved to W Corps Area N.S.C. (57c)	
N.S.C.16	18		Arrived New Area G.H.Q.m	
"	19		Lieut H.G. Brown & 95 O.R. left to form Troops at Q.8.A. Received S.A.A. and Grenades to complete establishment. Reinforcements P.10 Drawing	
P.11 a/5th	20		Horses to drawn P.B.A. (57c) Supplying S.A.A. to Infantry & Cavalry Brigade	
Q19b(57c)	21		Moved at 4.45am to A.18.B. (57c) Supplying Gun Ammunition to Batteries & S.A.A. to Infantry Brigade. Drawing Grenades etc. M. 1.A.A. Dump	
	22		Supplying Gun Ammunition to Batteries & S.A.A. to Infantry Brigade. Formed Dump at Havrincourt Wood	
	23		Supplying Gun Ammunition & S.A.A. to Infantry Brigade. Dump No. 2	

NOVEMBER 1917   ORIGINAL   62nd D.A.C.

Army Form C. 2118.

WAR DIARY
or
INTELLIGENCE SUMMARY.
(Erase heading not required.)

Place	Date	Hour	Summary of Events and Information	Remarks and references to Appendices
(MAP 57c) Q.19.d.43	24	8pm	Supplying Ammunition 2/Lieut Tempy Maj L.B. Bigg posted to D.A.C.	
	25		"	
	26		Supplying Ammunition. No 1 & 2 Sections moved to Frescate R.10.a.	
	27		" 1 & 2 Section moved to area K.3.9.b.c.	
	28		Supplying Ammunition. Sent 8 G.S. lorries & teams to Hermes under	
	28		Lieut L.B. Bigg to form part of H.A. Horse Amm Column	
	29		Supplying Ammunition. S.A.A. Lorry handed over to 47th Div. S.A.A. Section	
	29		47th Div Amm Column relieved S.A.A. Section 62 D.A.C. who moved to area R.25.b	
	30		Supplying Ammunition. HQ & No 3 Section shelled by various calibres	
	30		from 9am to 3pm. 1 Corporal killed. 1 O.R. wounded. 1 & 2 Sections	
	30		moved to area R.26 at midnight 29.11.17.	

Moonlow 1.6.
(m 4) 62 D.A.C.

T2134. Wt. W708—776. 500000. 4/16. Sir J.C. & S.

Secret

WO/12

Original

War Diary

of

62nd Divisional Ammunition Column

Volume XII

From 1st December 1917
To 31st December 1917

ORIGINAL

DECEMBER 1917

62nd D.A.C.

Army Form C. 2118.

WAR DIARY
or
INTELLIGENCE SUMMARY.
(Erase heading not required.)

Instructions regarding War Diaries and Intelligence Summaries are contained in F. S. Regs., Part II. and the Staff Manual respectively. Title pages will be prepared in manuscript.

Place	Date	Hour	Summary of Events and Information	Remarks and references to Appendices
(57c)				
Q.19.b.4.3	1st	8am	Supplying Ammunition - No 1 Section moved back to K.33.B.H.Q. shelled intermittently	day & night
"	2	"	Supplying Ammunition No 2 Section moved to K.22.B. H.Q. again shelled during the day	
P.22.d.4.7	2	"	H.Q. moved to P.22.d.4.7. 3rd & 4th Sections took up positions Protection	
"	3	"	"	
"	4	"	"	
"	5	"	" Moved 1.2.3 Sections to Area P.15 + 16	
"	6	"	"	
"	7	"	"	
"	8	"	Supplying Ammunition. Moved HQ. 1.2 + 3 Sections to Area Q.24. Central	
Q.24.Central	9	"	" Took over Dump at B.W.54 from Lieut Owen in charge. Sent 22 G.S. wagons to draw Rations for 59th Div	
"	10	"	Supplying Ammunition. 22 G.S. wagons drawing Rations for 59th Div	
"	11	"	" Handed over Dump B.W. 54 to 47 D.A.C.	[signature]
"	12	"	"	
"	13	"	"	
"	14	"	Supplying Ammunition. Took over Dump at Kebergues & took in charge [?] to near R.S. Proceeded to 2 Divs sent 12 wagons	

62nd D.A.C. ORIGINAL

DECEMBER 1917

Army Form C. 2118.

WAR DIARY
or
INTELLIGENCE SUMMARY.
(Erase heading not required.)

Place	Date	Hour	Summary of Events and Information	Remarks and references to Appendices
O.24 Central	15/1/17	8 am	Supplying Ammunition - Hd A.D.Hd	
"	6.12.17	"	" " Gwardgufflis.t	
			D.L. 62 D.A.	
I.27 Central	17.12.17		Supplying Ammunition	
"	19. "	"		
"	20. "	"	Capt M R Long returned from Hospital.	
"	21. "	"	J. Fraser Capt 25a	
"	22.12.17	"	Yatzgave for 2nd Division Artill	
	23.12.17	"	"	
	24.12.17	"	"	
	25.12.17	"	"	
	26.12.17	"	"	
	27.12.17	"	"	Gwarlwglis.t "Q"
	28.12.17	"	Moved to Echel. L Petit	D.L. 62

ORIGINAL

Army Form C. 2118.

WAR DIARY
or
INTELLIGENCE SUMMARY.
(Erase heading not required.)

Instructions regarding War Diaries and Intelligence Summaries are contained in F. S. Regs., Part II. and the Staff Manual respectively. Title pages will be prepared in manuscript.

Place	Date	Hour	Summary of Events and Information	Remarks and references to Appendices
G.14 Central	29.12.17	8pm	Moved to Tortequet.	
Louverne	30.12.17		Moved to Gouches Legal.	
	31.12.17		Army Intelpost to 62 Div. Requests that troops of D.A.C. section be notified.	

Gourdenblie Gt. Sgn
I.C. 62 D.A.C.

WAR DIARY

INTELLIGENCE SUMMARY

JANUARY 1918
Army Form C. 2118.
62 D Army Col
ORIGINAL

1. 62 D.A.C.

Place	Date	Hour	Summary of Events and Information	Remarks and references to Appendices
Jan 1 (note) Geophe Luye 1-19	9pm	Intelligence for Division		
	2/18		Sent 4 q.s. bergeon to 310 Brigade	
	3/18		Ye Eyene	
	4/18		"	
	5/18		Inspection by Army Commander (1st Army)	
	6/18		Ye Eyene	
	7/18		"	
	8/18		16 Officers & 62 O.R. to Boulogne to Reinforcements to 62 Div Arty. Took over following from them.	
			(A.A. Room at q. 11. C.6.3 (10 Offrs +150 OR) No 2 Troop at q. 9. d. 6. 8 (2 NCO + 8 Men) Esco	
	8/18		No 1 Dump at q. 9. d. 2. 8 (2 NCO + 4 Men) Also 518 horses	
	9/18		Ye Eyene	
	10/18		"	
	11/18		Reinforcements C of B. A. bergen to S.D.M. for Wicken F.	
	12/18		Ye Eyene Handed over temporary command to Capt Spencer	
	13/18		Yesterday 6.5 a.c.	

6 L.M. D.A.C.

WAR DIARY
INTELLIGENCE SUMMARY.
(Erase heading not required.)

Army Form C. 2118.

JANUARY 1918

ORIGINAL

Place	Date	Hour	Summary of Events and Information	Remarks and references to Appendices
GAUCHIN-LEGAL	13.1.18	8pm	Jalgune. 14 wagons to Brigade for move. 42 horses & 34 mules arrived	J.F.
LENS.11.4 1/10,000	14.1.18		Jalgune. 6 other ranks to dump to load from Base.	J.F.
	15.1.18		moved to ANZIN at G.11 central rf map 51.B.1.20000.	J.F.
ANZIN.	16.1.18		Supplying Ammn. 18 wagons on Jalgune. 10 drivers from Base	J.F.
R.f map	17.1.18		Inspection by C.R.A 20 " "	J.F.
51.B. G.7.D.5.7	18.1.18		Supplying Ammn. 28 " "	J.F.
	19.1.18		" " 28 " "	J.F.
	20.1.18		" " 44 " "	J.F.
	21.1.18		" " "	J.F.
	22.1.18		2/Lt. Kendall to S.A.A dump. 2/Lt. H.B. Jackson posted to 310 Bde	J.F.
			" Salvage. 30 wagons on Jalgune.	J.F.
	23.1.18		" 30 wagons on Jalgune.	J.F.
	24.1.18		Supplying Ammn. Salvage. 32 wagons on Jalgune.	J.F.
	25.1.18		" 30 "	J.F.
	26.1.18		1 Cert. 126 O.R. Indian Personnel joined and taken on strength accordingly. Inspection by the Divisional Commander	J.F.

(3) 62 DAC

WAR DIARY
INTELLIGENCE SUMMARY.
(Erase heading not required.)

JANUARY 1918   Army Form C. 2118.
ORIGINAL

Place	Date	Hour	Summary of Events and Information	Remarks and references to Appendices
G.2.D.5.7. 51.B.	27.1.18 28.1.18	8pm	Supplying Ammunition. Salvage. 968 Wagons on Fatigue. J.T. 25 - - - Commenced training of Indian Personnel. Lifted 16 wagons. Lt. Col. J.A. Woodcock returned from leave and assumed command. J.T. J. Laser Capt RFA 28 - 1 - 1918.	
	29.1.18		Supplying Ammunition. Salvage. 24 wagons on fatigue training Indian Personnel. Few	
	30.1.18		" 19 wagons on fatigue training Indian Personnel Few	
	30.1.18		Recd Recds S.A. holes to 312 Brigade R.F.A. few.	
	31.1.18		Supplying Ammunition. Salvage. 15 G.S. wagons on fatigue transferring Indian Remount.	
	31.1.18		2/Lieut E.J. Williams from 312 Brigade R.F.A. posted to No.1 Section Few.	

J.A. Woodcock Lieut Col. R.F.A.
Commdg 62 D.A.C.

Original.

Vol/4

<u>Confidential</u>

War Diary

of

62nd Div. Amm. Column.

Volume XIV

From. Feb. 1st. 1918.
To.   Feb. 28th. 1918.

6 Indl D.A.C.

FEBRUARY 1918

Army Form C. 2118.

WAR DIARY

INTELLIGENCE SUMMARY.
(Erase heading not required.)

ORIGINAL

Place	Date	Hour	Summary of Events and Information	Remarks and references to Appendices
G.H.Q Sheet 51 B	1.2.18	8 p.m	Supplying Ammunition & Fodder. 32 G.S. Wagons on Fatigue. Training Indian Personnel	See
	2.2.18		Supplying Ammunition & Fodder. 17 G.S. Wagons on Fatigue	"
"	3.2.18	"	" " " 10 G.S Wagons on Fatigue	" See
"	4.2.18	"	" " " 13 G.S Wagons on Fatigue	" See
"	5.2.18	"	" " " 20 G.S. Wagons on Fatigue	" See
"	5.2.18	"	G.O.C. 62 Div inspected Indian Personnel at Riding & Driving Drill	See
"	6.2.18	"	Supplying Ammunition & Fodder. 13 G.S. Wagons on Fatigue. Training Indian Personnel	See
"	7.2.18	"	" " " 26 G.S. Wagons on Fatigue	" See
"	8.2.18	"	" " " 19 G.S. Wagons on Fatigue	" See
"	8.2.18	"	Handed over S.A.A. Dump to 56 Div Arty.	See
"	9.2.18	"	Supplying Ammunition & Fodder. 17 G.S. Wagons on Fatigue. Training Indian Personnel	See
"	9.2.18	"	" " " 13 G.S. Wagons on Fatigue. Training Indian Personnel	See
"	10.2.18	"	1 N.C.O & 3 men with M. Ammunition Store at Vinigical. Saw	
"	11.2.18	"	Supplying Ammunition & Fodder. 26 G.S Wagons on Fatigue. Training Indian Personnel	See
"	11.2.18	"	Sent 1 N.C.O & 28 O.R to Boulogne to Remounts	See
"	12.2.18	"	Supplying Ammunition & Fodder. 17 G.S. Wagons on Fatigue. Training Indian Personnel	See

Army Form C. 2118.

WAR DIARY
or
INTELLIGENCE SUMMARY.
(Erase heading not required.)

Instructions regarding War Diaries and Intelligence Summaries are contained in F. S. Regs., Part II. and the Staff Manual respectively. Title pages will be prepared in manuscript.

Place	Date	Hour	Summary of Events and Information	Remarks and references to Appendices
Month of F.B.				
G.H.Q.	13.2.18		Supply Column - 15 G.S. Wagons in Fatigue. Training Indian Personnel.	See
	14.2.18		" 15 G.S. Wagons on Fatigue.	See
	15.2.18		" 12 F.L. Wagons on Fatigue. Handed 6 G.A.R. Pores to 66 Div. Arty.	See
Gun Hill H.Qrs. Gurkha Ropat	16.2.18		Moved to Gurkha Ropat. S.S. Renewals arrived. Training Indian Personnel.	Grace
	17.2.18		Sent 32 P.D. Horses & 10 Mules & 3 R. Horses. Training S. Renual Pers.	See
	18.2.18		Fatigues. 24 Indian Reinforcements arrived. Training Indian Personnel.	See
	19.2.18		Fatigues. "	See
	20.2.18		Fatigue. "	See
	21.2.18		Fatigue. "	See
	22.2.18		Fatigue. "	See
	23.2.18		Fatigue. "	See
	24.2.18		Fatigue. "	See
	25.2.18		Fatigue. "	See
	26.2.18		6 F.L. Wagons to 155 Army Bgde. R.F.A. Training Indian Personnel. 16"	See
	27.2.18		Fatigue. "	See
	28.2.18		Fatigue. "	See

T2134. Wt. W708—776. 500000. 4/15. Sir J. C. & S.

62nd Divisional Artillery

WAR DIARY

62nd DIVISIONAL AMMUNITION COLUMN R.F.A.

MARCH 1918

Original

WO/15

War Diary

of

62nd Divisional Ammunition Column

Volume VIX

From 1st March 1918
To 31st March 1918

Army Form C. 2118.

WAR DIARY
INTELLIGENCE SUMMARY.
(Erase heading not required.)

Place	Date	Hour	Summary of Events and Information	Remarks and references to Appendices
Gwoodenhof hult	1/3/18	8 pm	Training Section Personal	Saw
	2.3.18	"	" " "	"
	3.3.18	"	Yabgum. Sent 12 Mules to Brigade. Received 6 Mules to Remount Dept.	Saw
	4.3.18	"	" 10 G.S. Wagons to Brigade. 4 G.S. Wagons to D.Y.H.O. Training & Personnel	Saw
	5.3.18	"	Yabgum. 2 G.S. Wagons to D.Y.H.O. Training & Personnel	Saw
G.1.d.5.5.18	6.3.18	"	Moved to G.1.d.6.5. Sheet 5½.18 took over A.R.P. & L.G.A. During	Saw
	7.3.18	"	Supplying Ammunition & Salvage. 16 G.S. Wagons on fatigue. Training & Personnel the.	Saw
	8.3.18	"	" " " " 18 G.S. Wagons on fatigue " "	Saw
	9.3.18	"	" " " " 16 G.S. Wagons on fatigue " "	Saw
	10.3.18	"	Supplying Ammunition & Salvage. 18 G.S. Wagons on fatigue. Training & Personnel the.	Saw
	11.3.18	"	" " " " 18 G.S. Wagons on fatigue " "	Saw
	12.3.18	"	" " " " 20 G.S. Wagons on fatigue " "	Saw
	13.3.18	"	Supplying Ammunition & Salvage. 16 G.S. Wagons on fatigue. Training & Personnel the.	Saw
	14.3.18	"	" " " " 20 G.S. Wagons on fatigue " "	Saw

Gwoodenhofhult
Im by 62 D.C.

Army Form C. 2118.

WAR DIARY

INTELLIGENCE SUMMARY.
(Erase heading not required.)

OLYMPS MARCH 1918 ORIGINAL

Place	Date	Hour	Summary of Events and Information	Remarks and references to Appendices
(51B) B.1.d.65.15.3.18		8am	Supplying Ammunition & Salving. 14 G.S. wagons in Salagues	Free
	16.3.18		" " " 16 G.S. wagons in Salagues	Free
	17.3.18		" " " 12 G.S. wagons in Salagues	Free
	18.3.18		" " " 10 G.S. wagons in Salagues	Free
	19.3.18		" " " 19 G.S. wagons in Salagues	Free
	20.3.18		Supplying Ammunition & Salving. 11 G.S. wagons in Salagues	Free
	21.3.18		" " 14 G.S. wagons in Salagues	Free
	22.3.18		" " " Sent 3 P.G.S. wagons & 30 fly. Brigade for Stokes Mortars	Free
(51B) G.13.d.24.3.18 (57D)			Handed over R.R.P. to 2nd Cavalry D.A.C. Column marched to G.13.d (51B.)	Free
D.30.a.5.9.25.3.18			151mm marched to D.30.a.5.9 Supplying Ammunition	Free
(57D) D.15.49.27.3.18			Supplying Ammunition	Free
	28.3.18		Supplying Ammunition. Column marched to D.15.d.9.3 (57D)	Free
			Supplying Ammunition. Formed C.R.P. at D.23.a.5.0 (57D) Rear H.Q. Doer	Free
	29.3.18		Supplying Ammunition	Free
	30.3.18		Supplying Ammunition	Free
	31.3.18		Supplying Ammunition	Free

Greenfoot Roy Lt/Col
(comdg 62 D.A.C)

62nd Divisional Artilery

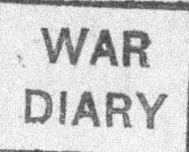

62nd DIVISIONAL AMMUNITION COLUMN R.F.A.

APRIL 1 9 1 8

Original.

Vol 16

War Diary

of

62nd. Div. Amm. Col.

Volume IV

From 1st April 1918
to 30th April 1918.

WAR DIARY

INTELLIGENCE SUMMARY

(Erase heading not required.)

Army Form C. 2118.

ORIGINAL

Place	Date	Hour	Summary of Events and Information	Remarks and references to Appendices
Sheet 57d. D.15 d 9.3/4-4.18 J.2 c 5.5	1.4.18	8 pm	Supplying Ammunition &c.	
	2.4.18		Supplying Ammunition. Handed A.P. Pour L.42 D&C Horsd to J.9.C.5.5 Established &c. A.R.P. and D. 26 Central Trin A.H. Quer in Charge &c.	
	2.4.18		Supplying Ammunition &c.	
	3.4.18		Supplying Ammunition &c.	
	4.4.18		Supplying Ammunition &c.	
	5.4.18		Supplying Ammunition. 8 G.S. Wagons on Fatigue &c.	
	6.4.18		Supplying Ammunition. 10 G.S. Wagons on Fatigue &c.	
	7.4.18		Supplying Ammunition. 12 G.S. Wagons on Fatigue &c.	
	8.4.18		Supplying Ammunition. 2 G.S. Wagons on Fatigue. Road & Corbon Sheer Not used at Sheer 6.212 6 got	
	9.4.18		Supplying Ammunition. 10 G.S. Wagons on Fatigue &c.	
	10.4.18		Supplying Ammunition &c.	
	11.4.18		Supplying Ammunition &c.	
	12.4.18		Supplying Ammunition. Handed over A.P.L.37 B.S.C. And 1 N.C.O 15 Men L.42 A.P.O. &c.	
	13.4.18		Supplying Ammunition &c.	
	14.4.18		Supplying Ammunition. 3 G.S. Wagons on Fatigue &c.	
	15.4.18		Supplying Ammunition. 12 G.S. Wagons on Fatigue &c.	
05/4/18			12 Drivers Posted to Brigade &c.	

J. Woodcock Lieut
4/62 D.A.C
(Acting O.C.)

Army Form C. 2118.

WAR DIARY
of
INTELLIGENCE SUMMARY.
(Erase heading not required.)

ORIGINAL

Instructions regarding War Diaries and Intelligence Summaries are contained in F. S. Regs., Part II. and the Staff Manual respectively. Title pages will be prepared in manuscript.

Place	Date	Hour	Summary of Events and Information	Remarks and references to Appendices
J.2.c.5.8.	16/4/18	8pm	Supplying Ammunition. Gas.	
	17/4/18		" " " "	
D.19.3.8.	18/4/18		" " " "	
	19/4/18		S.O.R. Loaded. 5 Mules killed 1 Wolseu Driver wound. 8.G.S. Murray & Hoskinson.	Moved to D.19.d.3.8. Took over Coys. Dev A.R.P.
	20/4/18		Supplying Ammunition. 20 Guerin horses & 312 Brigade R.Fd. 5 G.S. Wagon delivering Morter Ammunition	
	21/4/18		Supplying Ammunition. 1 O.R. wounded. 1 G.S. Wagon destroyed 1 Mule killed. 4 G.S. Wagons & Morter Ammunition	
	22/4/18		Supplying Ammunition.	
	23/4/18		" Staff of 9 to O.R. arrived for Brigade. Gas	
	23/4/18		Supplying Ammunition. Gas	
	"		" 5 G.S. Wagons on Falgun & Herlsan between fm 312 Bgde.	Gas
	24/4/18		S.A.A. Section move to Bois Palaiseau.	
	24/4/18		Supplying Ammunition. 1 Sgt + 200 O.R. 62 A.R.P.	Gas
	25/4/18		" Moved over 62 A.R.P. & 39 S.A.C. Lieut C.B. Bigg took over 62 A R.P.	
	26/4/18		Staff of 41 O.R. arrived for Brigade.	Gas
	"		Supplying Ammunition.	Gas
	"		" " "	
	28/4/18		Supplying Ammunition.	Gas
	29/4/18		" " Gas "	
	30/4/18		Supplying Ammunition. Pates & Steven to Brigade. Gas	

Original
Vol 17

Confidential

War Diary

of

62ⁿᵈ Divisional Ammunition Column

Volume XVII

From 1ˢᵗ May 1918
To 31ˢᵗ May 1918.

62ND D.A.C.
ORIGINAL

WAR DIARY
INTELLIGENCE SUMMARY
(Erase heading not required.)

MAY 1918.

Army Form C. 2118.

Instructions regarding War Diaries and Intelligence Summaries are contained in F.S. Regs., Part II. and the Staff Manual respectively. Title pages will be prepared in manuscript.

Place	Date	Hour	Summary of Events and Information	Remarks and references to Appendices
Huts 574 Hutton D.19.d.3.8.	1.5.18	8 am	Supplying Ammunition	
	2.5.18		"	
	3.5.18		Supplying Ammunition	
I.11.d.5.8.	4.5.18		" Owner moved to I.11.d.5.8. exchange of position with 37 D.A.C. Team	See Appendices
	5.5.18		" Handed temporary command of 310 Bn to Capt Stevens Muirfield	
	6/5/18		Supplying Amn. 24 L.D. Horses arrived 6 posted to 310 Bde 12 to 312 Bde.	dto
			W.L. JAMES 2/Lt. rejoined from 310 B de.	
	7/5/18		H.E. PARKINSON arrived off strength (medically boarded)	dto
			54 O.R. reinforcement arrived & sent to Brigades	
	8/8/18			dto
	9/5/18		5 R.G.A. Signallers sent to 310 Bde.	dto
	10/5/18		Lt Col F.A. Woodcock returned and resumed Command	

J. Fant Capt RFA

MAY 1918

62nd D.A.C.

Army Form C. 2118.

WAR DIARY
INTELLIGENCE SUMMARY.
(Erase heading not required.)

ORIGINAL

Instructions regarding War Diaries and Intelligence Summaries are contained in F.S. Regs., Part II. and the Staff Manual respectively. Title pages will be prepared in manuscript.

Place	Date	Hour	Summary of Events and Information	Remarks and references to Appendices
T.11.d.5.6.	11/5/18	8pm	Supplying Ammunition. 1 Officer & 290 O.Rs arrived from Base to Brigade. Rein. troops from 312 Bgde. to 62 D.A.C.	See
	12/5/18		Supplying Ammunition. 80 O.Rs from Base to Brigade.	See
	13/5/18		Supplying Ammunition. Lieut H. Sorrett posted to 312 Bgde. 2/Lt E. Goodliam posted to 312 Bgde.	See
	14/5/18		Supplying Ammunition.	See
	15/5/18		Supplying Ammunition. 6 G.S. wagons in Salvage.	See
	16/5/18		Supplying Ammunition. Lieut W.E. Hotchen posted from 310 Brigade to 62 D.A.C.	See
	17/5/18		S.A.A. arrived from Base to Brigade. D.A.A. Section moved to Henu. D.19 central.	See
	18/5/18		Supplying Ammunition. Delivering Returns to Y Horlies.	See
	19/5/18		Supplying Ammunition. 4 G.S. wagons in Salvage. Delivering Returns to Y Horlies.	See
	20/5/18		Supplying Ammunition Coln. Handed over Explosive, wagon & team from H.Q. & L.A.A. Section, reprs.	See
	21/5/18		Supplying Ammunition. Delivering Return to Y Horlies.	See
	22/5/18		Supplying Ammunition. 48 O.Rs arrived from Base to Brigade.	See
	23/5/18		"	See
	24/5/18		"	See
	25/5/18		Supplying Ammunition. 80 O.Rs arrived from Base posted 7 to Bgde. 1 to D.A.C. G.O.C. R.A inspected H.Q. & No. 1 & 2 Sections. Succeeded Lt. Col. Crowley 62 Div. C.	See

62nd D.A.C.
Army Form C. 2118.

MAY 1918

WAR DIARY
or
INTELLIGENCE SUMMARY.
(Erase heading not required.)

Instructions regarding War Diaries and Intelligence Summaries are contained in F. S. Regs., Part II. and the Staff Manual respectively. Title pages will be prepared in manuscript.

ORIGINAL

Place	Date	Hour	Summary of Events and Information	Remarks and references to Appendices
I.U.S.B	26/5/18		Supplying Ammunition, Delivering H.M. Rations 2b.ORep Base posted 316 Bgde + 151 B/AC	Steen
	27/5/18		" " 2.OR from Base posted to DAC 2/Lt of Rees posted to H/Al posted	Steen
	28/5/18		Supplying Ammunition & Delivering H.M. Rations	Steen
	29/5/18		" " G.O.C. 62 Div Inspected H.Q. NE 1 + 2 Sections	Steen
	30/5/18		Supplying Ammunition + Delivering H.M. Rations	Steen
	31/5/18		Supplying Ammunition + Delivering H.M. Rations	Steen

Lieut Col Comdr
62nd D.A.C.

Original
Vol 18

War Diary

of

62nd Divisional Ammunition Column

Volume VI

From 1st June 1918
To 30th June 1918

WAR DIARY
or
INTELLIGENCE SUMMARY.

(Erase heading not required.)

62ND D.A.C. Army Form C. 2118.

ORIGINAL

JUNE 1918

Place	Date	Hour	Summary of Events and Information	Remarks and references to Appendices
Sheet 57D 1/20,000				
I.n.A.S. 8	1/6/18	8 p.m.	Supplying Ammunition & return T.M. Rations	See.
	2/6/18	8 p.m.	"	See.
	3/6/18	8 p.m.	"	See.
	4/6/18	8 p.m.	2/Lt. B.G. Thomas posted from 3rd A.F.A. Bde.	See.
	5/6/18	8 p.m.	"	See.
	6/6/18	8 p.m.	"	See.
	6/6/18	6 p.m.	"	See.
	7/6/18	8 p.m.	"	See.
	8/6/18	8 p.m.	Capt. Licht-Elliot reverts to Indian Remount. 2/Lt. O.S. Rogers to goes to No. 1 Section. 2/Lt. H.C. Markham from No. 1 Sec. to No. 3 Section	See.
	9/6/18	8 p.m.	"	See.
	10/6/18	8 p.m.	"	See.
	11/6/18	8 p.m.	"	See.
	12/6/18	8 p.m.	"	See.
	13/6/18	8 p.m.	"	See.
	14/6/18	8 p.m.	"	See.
	15/6/18	8 p.m.	"	See.
	16/6/18	8 p.m.	"	See.
	17/6/18	8 p.m.	"	See.

JUNE 1918

62ND DAC Army Form C. 2118.

ORIGINAL

WAR DIARY

INTELLIGENCE SUMMARY.
(Erase heading not required.)

Place	Date	Hour	Summary of Events and Information	Remarks and references to Appendices
Bhd. 57.D 1/40000				
	18/6/18	8 p.m.	2.11 A.S. 8. Suspending Ammunition soliciting T.M. Relieving Reorganised Eeff.d F.N.1+2 Reclaim	See
	19.6.18	"	" 38 Drivers +51 P.B. Animals taken to Bapaume	
	20.6.18	"	"	
	21.6.18	"	" 12 Drivers posted to Reinforcement Camp	See
	22.6.18	"	"	See
	23.6.18	"	"	See
	24.6.18	"	"	See
	25.6.18	"	"	See
	26.6.18	"	"	See
Bhd. 57.D Quarto Amplier	27.6.18	"	In reserve	See
	28.6.18	"	"	See
	29.6.18	"	" Commenced return of General Gunnery	See
	30/6/18	"	" 13 O.Rs from Reserve 3.C. Brigade. 7 to F.A. B's. 1 to D.A.C.	See

J. Woodcock Lieut Col. R.A.
(comdg 62. D.A.C.)

Divl. Artillery

62nd Division.

62nd DIVISIONAL AMMUNITION COLUMN,

J U L Y, 1 9 1 8.

JULY 1918.

WAR DIARY
INTELLIGENCE SUMMARY.

(Erase heading not required.)

Army Form C. 2118.

62ND D.A.C.

ORIGINAL

Place	Date	Hour	Summary of Events and Information	Remarks and references to Appendices
Sheet 57F I/50,000 AMPLIER	1/7/18	8 pm	In reserve training + drilling	Faco
	2/7/15	8 pm	"	Faco
	3/7/15	8 pm	"	Faco
	4/7/15	8 pm	"	Faco
	5/7/15	8 pm	"	Faco
	6/7/15	8 pm	6.O.R. Reinforcement arrived	Faco
	7/7/18	8 pm	Lieut. Col. F.A. WOODCOCK D.S.O. admitted to Hospital	Faco
	8/7/18	8 pm	M.S.M. awarded to 42730 B.S.M. WALSH.A.P. Battery 3/7/18	Faco
	9/7/18	8 pm	Lieut Col F.A. WOODCOCK D.S.O returned from Hospital	Faco
	10/7/18	8 pm	"	Faco
	11/7/18	8 pm	"	Faco
	12/7/18	8 pm	"	Faco
	13/7/18	8 pm	"	Faco
	14/7/18	8 pm	"	Faco
	15/7/18	8 pm	"	Faco
	16/7/18	8 pm	"	Faco
	17/7/18	8 pm	"	Faco
	18/7/18	8 pm	Entrained at DOULLENS to join 22ND CORPS	Faco

JULY 1918

62ND D.A.C.

Army Form C. 2118.

ORIGINAL

WAR DIARY
or
INTELLIGENCE SUMMARY.
(Erase heading not required.)

Instructions regarding War Diaries and Intelligence Summaries are contained in F. S. Regs., Part II. and the Staff Manual respectively. Title pages will be prepared in manuscript.

Place	Date	Hour	Summary of Events and Information	Remarks and references to Appendices
Sheet 1/50,000 17/				
CHALLONS	1/15	7pm	detrained ARCY-SUR-AUBE marched to MAILLY arrived at 7pm.	taco
	15/7/15	3pm	left MAILLY 9AM marched to VOOZY arrived 6pm	taco
	19/7/15	5pm	left VOOZY 9.30AM marched to FONTAINE arrived 9pm	taco
Sheet 34. 1/50,000	20/7/15	9pm	left FONTAINE an SAA section and took up Batth. position at FORET-DE-LA-MONTAGNE.	taco
REIMS			established ammunition supply. Took over Railhead Dump GERMAINE. Horse Transport	taco
			attached to D.A.C. 3 Officers 82 O.R. attached from T.M. BATTERIES.	taco
	21/7/15	8pm	Supplying ammunition + delivering T.M.B Rations established ARP (head. WRANGLE?)	taco
			at old roads N.W. of D.A.C. (de MONT. RIEUL)	taco
	22/7/15	7pm	Supplying Ammunition and delivering T.M. Rations	taco
	23/7/15	8pm	"	taco
	24/7/15	7pm	" Heavy bombardment by enemy airmen	taco
			" "36 Animals killed 30 Animals + 3 O.R. wounded	taco
			" "D.A.C. Leon SAA Section moved to	taco
			" "PIE-DE-BOEUFS, 2 OFFICERS and	taco
	25/7/15	7pm	15 O.R. Reinforcement arrived attacks to SAA Section. 16 O.R. dispatch to 310 + 312 Bts	taco
	26/7/15	5pm	6 Indian Reinforcement arrived posted to SAA Section	taco
	27/7/15	5pm	Supplying Ammunition + delivering T.M. Rations	taco

Army Form C. 2118.

62nd DAC

WAR DIARY
or
INTELLIGENCE SUMMARY.
(Erase heading not required.)

ORIGINAL

JULY 1915

Instructions regarding War Diaries and Intelligence Summaries are contained in F. S. Regs., Part II. and the Staff Manual respectively. Title pages will be prepared in manuscript.

Place	Date	Hour	Summary of Events and Information	Remarks and references to Appendices
Sect 54	26/7/15	8pm	Supplying Ammn + delivering TM Rations. DAC. HQ moved to the E in FORET-DE-LA-MONTAGNE	See
15000			1st Section at 224·7 - 267·3 + ARP moved to 223·7 - 267·7	See
	29/7/15	8pm	Supplying Ammunition + delivering TM Rations	See
REIMS	30/7/15	8pm	Recvd orders to entrain N° 1 Section depots for CHALONS at 3pm	See
	31/7/15	3pm	Marched to AIGNY and at 3pm two SAA sections then ARP & Ammunition	See

Second of Field
(under 62. D.A.C)

T2134. Wt. W708—776. 500000. 4/15. Sir J. C. & S.

Original

Vol 18

War Diary.

62nd Divisional
Trench Mortar Btties

Volume XX

From August 1st 1918
To August 31st 1918

C.R. Bottomley, Captain R.F.A.
D.T.M.O 62nd Division

Sept 4th 18

Original

WAR DIARY
or
INTELLIGENCE SUMMARY
(Erase heading not required.)

Army Form C. 2118.

Trench Mortar Btties
62nd Division

Volume 8

Instructions regarding War Diaries and Intelligence Summaries are contained in F.S. Regs., Part II. and the Staff Manual respectively. Title pages will be prepared in manuscript.

Place	Date	Hour	Summary of Events and Information	Remarks and references to Appendices
AUTHIE (ADRAN CROSS ROADS)	August 1st 1918		X/62 arrived AUTHIE from French Army Area	GRB
PLIVOT	2nd		X/62 moved with S.A.A. Section 62nd D.A.C. by road to PLIVOT	GRB
"	3rd		Nothing to report	GRB
"			X/62 moved with S.A.A. Section 62nd D.A.C. by road to FERE CHAMPENOISE entraining there for in Corps Area	GRB
AUTHIE	5th		X/62 arrived at AUTHIE	GRB
"	6th to 16th		Both batteries training. An experimental dud was laid near AUTHIE and engaged by aeroplanes	GRB
"	17th		Nothing to report	GRB
"	18th to 20th		Both batteries moved up and built positions near BUCQUOY.	GRB GRB
BUCQUOY	21st		Batteries co-operated with other Artillery in Barrage preceding attack on BUCQUOY, firing nearly 200 rounds.	GRB
"	22nd		Personnel resting on 3%s A.R.R.	GRB
"	23rd to 25th		Nothing to report	GRB
"	26th		Personnel withdrawn to AUTHIE	GRB
AUTHIE	31st		Both batteries moved by road to COMIECOURT.	GRB

GRBullinley
D.T.M.O. 62nd Division
Capt RFA

Secret   Original

War Diary

of

62nd Divisional Ammunition Column

Volume ~~**~~ XXI

From 1st September 1918
To 30th September 1918

WAR DIARY or INTELLIGENCE SUMMARY.

SEPTEMBER 1918   Army Form C. 2118.   ORIGINAL

Place	Date	Hour	Summary of Events and Information	Remarks and references to Appendices
Rci Map 5/2 Jul. OCC S.14.C.2.4.	1/9/18	7pm	Supplying Ammunition 5 Gunner and 5 Thorn r de Signallers to 310 Bt. to replace casualties.	See
	2/9/18	8pm	"	See
	3/9/18	5am	" DAC two SAA Section return to S.10.a.4.4 at JAMES attached to B/310	See
	4/9/18	8pm	" Lieut W.H. HOUSE M.O. awarded the M.C.	See
	5/9/18	8pm	" Above 10. O.R. reinforcement arrived posts as follows 2 to 310 Bt. 3 " 312 " M.A.C.	See
	6/9/18	8pm	" 2 " " to 310 Bt.	See
	7/9/18	7pm	" 6 Gunner from No.2 section to B/310 to replace casualties	See
	8/9/18	7am	"	See
	9/9/18	8am	DAC less SAA A Section move to A.19.6 and approve the Division	See
	10/9/18	8am	" I st section at 8am establish AP Pa at VELU T.15.a.3.3	See
			and BERTINCOURT P.7.c.6.2. Supplying Ammunition SAA Section move to T.3.4.c. Moeuvres line Thu	
	10/9/18	8pm	Supplying Ammunition Sg. O.R. reinforcement arrived posted as follows 5 " D.A.C. 20 " 310 Bt. 3 " D.A.C.	See
			Reinforcement arrived and posted 2 to 310 Bt. 3 " M.A.C.	See
	11/9/18	8am	"	See
	12/9/18	8pm	" 2b O.R. reinforcement arrived posted 4 to 310 Bt.	See
			"	See
	13/9/18	7pm	Lieut L. WILSON returned from leave	See
	14/9/18	8pm	"	See

signed (illegible) Lt Col
(comdg) D.D.A.C.

SEPTEMBER 1918

Army Form C. 2118.

WAR DIARY or INTELLIGENCE SUMMARY.

(Erase heading not required.)

ORIGINAL

Instructions regarding War Diaries and Intelligence Summaries are contained in F. S. Regs., Part II. and the Staff Manual respectively. Title pages will be prepared in manuscript.

Place	Date	Hour	Summary of Events and Information	Remarks and references to Appendices
Ref. Map 5/c 1/20,000	15/9/18	8 pm	Supplying Ammunition. Attack by Enemy Aircraft. 1 G' Killed, E.O. + 8 OR wounded	See
I.L. Ambul	16/9/18	5 pm	SAA section went to M.O.R.K. H.q.o. contact. DAC under orders of 3"DA supplying Ammunition	See
	17/9/18	8 pm	Supplying Ammunition. Handed over VIII A.R.P. to 3" IIAC.	See
	18/9/18	8 pm	" Delivering J.M. Rations. 1 Br. Reinforcement posted to 310 Bgde	See
	19/9/18	8 am	15 Brs. Reinforcements arrived 10 to 310 - 2 to 312 - 2 to No.2 & 1 to No.1 Section	See
			Supplying Ammunition. Delivery J.M. Rations. Cpl. V.H.S. Long proceeded on leave. Lt. Curzon assumed duties of Adjutant.	See
	20/9/18	8 am	Supplying Rations. Delivering J.M. Rations. 1 Indian OR accidently injured	See
	21/9/18	8 am	Supplying Ammunition. Delivering J.M. Rations.	See
	22/9/18	8 am	" Delivering J.M. Rations. 12 Indian OR's arrived - Posted to No.3 Section	See
			1 Horse Remount arrived for Adjutant.	See
	23/9/18	8 am	Supplying Ammunition. Delivering J.M. Rations.	See
	24/9/18	8 am	" " "	See
	25/9/18	8 am	" " Forward A.R.P. established at J.35.d.27.	See
			under Sergt. Russell (9th.) 4 Reinforcements arrived. Posted - 1 to 310 Bgde.	See
			19 to 312 Bgde. 8 to 1st Battalion.	See
			Montenoff (61295th D.A.C.)	See
			(moved to 310 D.A.C.)	See

WAR DIARY
or
INTELLIGENCE SUMMARY.
(Erase heading not required.)

Army Form C. 2118.

Instructions regarding War Diaries and Intelligence Summaries are contained in F. S. Regs., Part II. and the Staff Manual respectively. Title pages will be prepared in manuscript.

Place	Date	Hour	Summary of Events and Information	Remarks and references to Appendices
	1918			
	26/9/18	8 pm	Supplying Ammunition. Delivering S.A.A. Rations	See
	27/9/18	8 pm	" " " "	See
			S.A.B. hrs S.A.A. station moved to Q.b.6.9 (A.A. station came under Q Shell). 1 O.R. wounded.	See
	28/9/18	8 pm	Dump at 135d 27 shelled & ammunition lost. New dump opened at Q2c49. Hr.Wagons in stage supplying rations. Delivering S.M. Rations. 2 Lorries taken to 10M for repairs.	See
	29/9/18	8 pm	Supplying Ammunition. Delivering S.M. Rations. S.A.B. this A.A. station moved to N.2.9.9 (57c.4)0000.	See
	30/9/18	8 pm	Supplying Ammunition. Delivering S.M. Rations. New APP to K26 & 19. Lt. Wrangler Vacc. 3 Lorries taken to 10M.	See

Signed R.G.S. Pte
Comdg 62 D.A.C.

Secret.   Original

War Diary

of

62nd Divisional Ammunition Column

Volume XXII

From 1st October 1918
To 31st October 1918

Army Form C. 2118.

OCTOBER.

WAR DIARY
or
INTELLIGENCE SUMMARY.

(Erase heading not required.)

ORIGINAL

Instructions regarding War Diaries and Intelligence Summaries are contained in F. S. Regs., Part II. and the Staff Manual respectively. Title pages will be prepared in manuscript.

Place	Date	Hour	Summary of Events and Information	Remarks and references to Appendices
59 C. 1000.0.0.	1918 Oct 1	8 am	Supplying Ammunition. Delivering I.M. Rations.	Nil
	2	8 am	do. do. 3 Guns taken to 10M. A.R.P. at 22.c.4.9	Nil
			Shied and ammunition stored.	Nil
	3	8 am	Supplying Ammunition. Delivering I.M. Rations. Capt. J. Fraser proceeded on leave.	Nil
	4	8 am	do. do. 29 Reinforcements arrived. Posted 8 to 310	Nil
			18 to 312, 3 to D.A.C.	Nil
5		8 am	Supplying Ammunition. Delivering I.M. Rations. Ralls erected (Called Div. Arty).	Nil
	6	8 am	do do do. Capt. D.H.S. Long returned from leave.	Nil
	7	8 am	do. do. to Capt. J.H.S. Long att'd H.Q. 62nd D.A.	Nil
	8	8 am	do. do. 36 Brit'sh Reinforcements arrived. Posted 22 to 310	Nil
			4 to 312. 5 Indian Reinforcements arrived. Posted 4 to No 1 Sec. 1 to No 3 Sec.	Nil
9		8 am	Supplying Ammunition. Delivering I.M. Rations. New Appendtablished at 130a.36.	Nil
			H.Q. D.A.B. moved to L29.b.35. Sec 1 + 2 sections under orders of 310	Nil
57 B. 4000.			+ 312. Cycles. No 1.x moved to H.27.L.88 (57 B) # 5 to	Nil
	10	8 am	Supplying Ammunition. Delivering I.M. Rations. No.2 Sec. moved to G.2.d & 81.	Nil

T2134. Wt. W708—776. 500000. 4/15. Sir J. C. & S.

OCTOBER

WAR DIARY
or
INTELLIGENCE SUMMARY.

Army Form C. 2118.

ORIGINAL

Place	Date	Hour	Summary of Events and Information	Remarks and references to Appendices
57 C.9.	1918			
	Oct 11	8am	Delivering Ammunition. H.Q. D.A.C. moved to G.30.c.63. A.R.P. closed. 28 Reinforcements	two
			arrived. Could 10 to 310 - 10 to 312 - 4 to 4x.x - 4 to 40.2x.	two
	12	8am	Supplying Ammunition. Delivering T.M. Rations	two
	13	8am	H.Q. & No. 2x moved to H.12.a.18. Hdx moved to G.28.b.91.	two
	14	6am	Delivering Ammunition and Delivering T.M. Rations	two
	15	8am	Delivering Ammunition and Delivering T.M. Rations	two
	16	6am	A.R.P. Established at J.2.b.9.1. Lieut. Owen 1/c.	two
	16	10am	Lieut. Penroth assumes duties of acting adjutant. 2nd Lieut. Rew joined	two
	16	5am	to 310th Brigade R.F.A. Supplying Ammunition and Delivering T.M. Rations	two
	17	6am	Supplying Ammunition and Delivering T.M. Rations	two
	17	6pm	No 2 Section D.A.C. moved to G.28.d.9.9. 2 O.R. wounded	two
	18	8am	One O.R. hulk killed by shell fire	two
	18	8am	Supplying Ammunition and Delivering T.M. Rations	two
	19	6am	moved to C.23.C. 20 Reinforcements arrived and joined	two
	19	6am	Q.5 to 310th Brigade R.F.A. 6 to 312 Brigade R.F.A. 5 to D.A.C.	two
	19	6am	Supplying Ammunition and Delivering T.M. Rations	two

Army Form C. 2118.

WAR DIARY
or
INTELLIGENCE SUMMARY.
(Erase heading not required.)

ORIGINAL

OCTOBER

Instructions regarding War Diaries and Intelligence Summaries are contained in F. S. Regs., Part II. and the Staff Manual respectively. Title pages will be prepared in manuscript.

Place	Date	Hour	Summary of Events and Information	Remarks and references to Appendices
S.W.B.	1918			
	Oct 20	8am	Supplying Ammunition Delivering T.M. Rations to A.R.P. Establishing new A.R.P. Establishing at D.14.a.6.2. Lieut Owen i/charge of A.R.P. Lead.	Itinero
			Reinforcements arrived and Lectd. 5 to 312 Brigade R.F.A. H.	Itinero
			13 to 310 Brigade R.F.A. H to Trench Mortar Battery 3. 16 Remounts	Itinero
			arrived and Lectd to D.A.C.	Itinero
	21	8am	Supplying Ammunition and Delivering T.M. Rations	Itinero
	22	8am	Supplying Ammunition and Delivering T.M. Rations. Capt. I. Fraser	Itinero
			returned from Leave	Itinero
	23	8am	Supplying Ammunition and Delivering T.M. Rations	Itinero
	24	8am	D.A.C. less S.A.A. Section moved to:- Head Quarters D.6.a.5.8. Nos 1 & 2	Itinero
			Sections to D.5.c.9.6. Capt. I. Fraser evacuated to Hospital.	Itinero
	25	8am	Supplying Ammunition and Delivering T.M. Rations. 1 O.R. transferred	Itinero
			to W.J. Field f.c.	Itinero
	26	8am	Supplying Ammunition and Delivering T.M. Rations S.A.A. Section	Itinero
			moved to D.5.b.9.9. 20 Reinforcements arrived and Lectd	Itinero
			to 3rd Brigade R.F.A. Lieut Chas. assumes Command of No 2 Section	Itinero

Army Form C. 2118.

ORIGINAL

OCTOBER. WAR DIARY or INTELLIGENCE SUMMARY.

(Erase heading not required.)

Instructions regarding War Diaries and Intelligence Summaries are contained in F. S. Regs, Part II. and the Staff Manual respectively. Title pages will be prepared in manuscript.

Place	Date	Hour	Summary of Events and Information	Remarks and references to Appendices
51B	1918			
	Oct 27	8am	Salving Ammunition and Delivering T.M. Rations	Two
	28	6pm	Salving Ammunition and Delivering T.M. Rations. To 496,460 Sept.	Two
			MALLINSON. G and to 496,893 Pts MARTIN.W.J. awarded the M. Medal.	Two
	29	8am	Salving Ammunition and Delivering T.M. Rations. Inspection of Clothing and Equipment by Commanding Officer.	Two
	30	8am	Salving Ammunition Delivering T.M. Rations.	Two
	31	8pm	Salving Ammunition Delivering T.M. Rations	Two

Sneadshefes/Bgt/ Two
Commdg 62 Div
Coy MT AsC

Secret
WD 23

Original

War Diary

of

62nd Divisional Ammunition Column

Volume XXIII

From 1st November 1918
To 30th November 1918

ORIGINAL.

WAR DIARY
or
INTELLIGENCE SUMMARY.
(Erase heading not required.)

Army Form C. 2118.

62nd D.A.C.

NOVEMBER.

Instructions regarding War Diaries and Intelligence Summaries are contained in F. S. Regs., Part II. and the Staff Manual respectively. Title pages will be prepared in manuscript.

Place	Date	Hour	Summary of Events and Information	Remarks and references to Appendices
MAP 51B 1/40,000	1/11/15	8 am	A.R.P. established at W.9.c.3.7. (51a) Lieut Owen to Area Commandant. H. Wieux. Lieut James assumed command of No.2 Section. Lieut. Colonel F.C. Woodcock D.S.O. proceeded on leave to Paris. Capt. Keiley assumed command of D.A.C. No. 790551. Sgt. W. LACEY. No. 715055 Bdr A. FIRTH awarded "Military Medal". Delivering T.M. Rations. Supplying Ammunition.	Two Two Two Two Two
	2/11/15	8 pm	A.R.P. established at R.31.CENTRAL (51a) Lieut H. Meacham relieved from leave and assumed command of No.2 Section. Supplying Ammunition. Delivering T.M. Rations. 2 other ranks wounded and one mule killed by shell fire.	Two Two Two Two
MAP 51A 1/40,000	3/11/15	8 pm	D.A.C. less S.A.A. Section moved to W.9.c.3.7. S.A.A. Section came under direct orders of "Q" DIVISION. Supplying Ammunition. Delivering T.M. Rations. Hostile shelling, 1 mule wounded. D.A.C. less S.A.A. Section moved to R.31.CENTRAL. A.R.P. opened at R.16.c.5.9. Lieut Owen to.	Two Two Two Two
	4/11/15	8 am	Supplying Ammunition. Delivering T.M. Rations.	Two
MAP 51 1/40,000	5/11/15	8 pm	D.A.C. less S.A.A. Section moved to M.10.d.3.7. A.R.P. established at M.16.c.4.5. Supplying Ammunition. Delivering T.M. Rations. Heavy Hostile shelling during the night.	Two Two Two
	6/11/15	8 pm	Lieut Colonel Woodcock D.S.O. returned from leave and re-assumed command of D.A.C. Supplying Ammunition and delivering T.M. Rations	Two Two

Forward

ORIGINAL

Army Form C. 2118.

WAR DIARY

INTELLIGENCE SUMMARY.

(Erase heading not required.)

62nd D.A.C

NOVEMBER

Place	Date	Hour	Summary of Events and Information	Remarks and references to Appendices
MAP. 51 1/40,000	7/11/15	8.4 p.m.	A.R.P. opened at N.15 CENTRAL. Capt. T.C. KEMLEY proceeded on leave. Lieut. Wilson assumed command of No.1 Section. A.R.P. at R16.d. handed over to M.T. Company. A.R.P at N.9.c.3.2. closed. Supplying ammunition and delivering T.M. rations.	Nil
	8/11/15	8.4 p.m.	Supplying ammunition. Delivering T.M. Rations. D.A.C less S.A.A Section moved to N.15.a.4.4 A.R.P. opened at M.2H.CENTRAL. A.R.P at M.16.6.4.5 taken over by Corps	Nil Nil Nil
	9/11/15	8 p.m.	Supplying ammunition. Delivering T.M. Rations. D.A.C less S.A.A. Section moved to :- HEADQUARTERS:- O.16.C.4.7 18.2. SECTIONS:- O.22.C.4.7	Nil Nil
	10/11/15	8 a.m.	A.R.P. opened at O.22.a.3.1. Supplying ammunition. Delivering T.M. Rations. Capt. Thorpe rejoined D.A.C from hospital and assumed command of No.2 Section.	Nil Nil
	11/11/15	5 a.m. 11 a.m.	Hostilities cease at 11am. D.A.C. less S.A.A. Section moved to P.16.c.7.5. All A.R.Ps closed. Delivering T.M. Rations. Lieut. H.A Owen attached to No.1. Section.	Nil Nil
	12/11/15	8 p.m.	Supplied 30 Wagons for Infantry Rations. Lieut Owen rejoined No 2 Section. Lieut CO Badham-Jackson posted to No.1. SECTION	Nil
	13/11/15	5 p.m.	Resting and cleaning Wagons, Harness etc	Nil
	14/11/15	5 p.m.	2 Sergeants reinforcements arrived and posted to 3rd a Brigade. 96 OR reinforcements arrived and posted as follows:- 2nd Bde = 40, 310 Bde = 38, D.T.M.O = 15, D.A.C = 3	Nil

ORIGINAL.

Army Form C. 2118.

WAR DIARY
INTELLIGENCE SUMMARY.
(Erase heading not required.)

62nd DAC

NOVEMBER.

Instructions regarding War Diaries and Intelligence Summaries are contained in F. S. Regs., Part II. and the Staff Manual respectively. Title pages will be prepared in manuscript.

Place	Date	Hour	Summary of Events and Information	Remarks and references to Appendices
MAP 51 1/100 000	15/11	8pm	Resting, cleaning Wagons, Harness, etc.	See
	16/11	8pm	DAC moved to Q11.d.9.9. CAPTAIN V.H.S. LONG rejoined from attachment to H.Q.R.A.	See
			LIEUT KEMSETT rejoined S.A.A. Section.	See
	17/11	8pm	LIEUT H. LEE proceeded on leave. 50 Remounts arrived and posted:- 26- No.1 Section- 24- No 2 Section	See
	18/11	8pm	Resting, cleaning Wagons, Harness etc.	See
MAP. HIRSON-8. 1/100 000	19/11	8pm	DAC moved to SOLRE-SUR-SAMBRE.	See
	20/11	8pm	DAC moved to BERZEE.	See
	21/11	8pm	Resting cleaning Wagons Harness etc.	See
	22/11	8pm	ditto	See
	23/11	8pm	ditto	See
			D.A.C Sports held at BERZEE	See
	24/11	8pm	DAC moved to HANZINNE.	See
	25/11	8pm	DAC moved to BIESMEREE.	See
	26/11	5pm	DAC moved to:- HQ MARTEAU. Nos 1 & 3 Sections:- SOSOYE. No 2 Section:- FALAEN STATION	See
			CAPT T.C KEVNEY returned from leave. SERGT W. MATNEY awarded bar to MILITARY MEDAL	See
	27/11	8pm	DAC moved to LISOGNE.	See
	28/11	8pm	Resting, cleaning Wagons, Harness etc.	See

ORIGINAL.

Army Form C. 2118.

WAR DIARY
or
INTELLIGENCE SUMMARY.
(Erase heading not required.)

62nd D.A.C.

NOVEMBER

Instructions regarding War Diaries and Intelligence Summaries are contained in F. S. Regs., Part II. and the Staff Manual respectively. Title pages will be prepared in manuscript.

Place	Date	Hour	Summary of Events and Information	Remarks and references to Appendices
Maps:- Hazebrouck 1/100 000	1915 29/11	8 pm	Resting, cleaning Wagons, Harness &c.	See
	30/11	8 am	Resting, cleaning Wagons, Harness &c.	See

Luscombe
Lieut. Colonel
Commanding. 62nd (WR) D.A.C.

"Secret."   Original.

War Diary
of
62ⁿᵈ Divisional Ammunition Column.

Volume ~~XII~~
XXIV

From 1st December 1918.
To 31st December 1918.

ORIGINAL.

WAR DIARY
or
INTELLIGENCE SUMMARY.
(Erase heading not required.)

Army Form C. 2118.

DECEMBER.

Instructions regarding War Diaries and Intelligence Summaries are contained in F. S. Regs., Part II. and the Staff Manual respectively. Title pages will be prepared in manuscript.

Place	Date	Hour	Summary of Events and Information	Remarks and references to Appendices
MAP MAZUR 8 1/100,000 1:50,000	1916			
	DEC.1	8pm	Resting and cleaning up Harness Equipment etc	Yes
	2	8pm	Resting and cleaning up Harness Equipment etc	Yes
	3	8pm	Resting and cleaning up Harness Equipment etc	Yes
	4	8pm	Resting and cleaning up Harness Equipment etc	Yes
	5	8pm	Resting and cleaning up Harness Equipment etc	Yes
	6	8pm	Resting and cleaning up Harness Equipment etc	Yes
	7	8pm	Resting and cleaning up Harness Equipment etc	Yes
	8	8pm	Resting and cleaning up Harness Equipment etc	Yes
	9	8pm	Resting and cleaning up Harness Equipment etc	Yes
MAP TARCOYNE 1/100,000	10	8pm	D.A.C. marched to LEIGNON.	Yes
	11	8pm	D.A.C. marched to PORCHERESSE	Yes
	12	8pm	D.A.C. marched to BONSIN	Yes
	13	8pm	D.A.C. marched to FILOT	Yes
	14	8pm	D.A.C. marched to TAHIER	Yes
	15	8pm	Resting and cleaning up Harness Equipment etc	Yes
	16	8pm	D.A.C. marched to TROIS PONT.	Yes

ORIGINAL.

Army Form C. 2118.

Instructions regarding War Diaries and Intelligence
Summaries are contained in F.S. Regs., Part II.
and the Staff Manual respectively. Title pages
will be prepared in manuscript.

WAR DIARY
or
INTELLIGENCE SUMMARY.
(Erase heading not required.)

DECEMBER.

Place	Date	Hour	Summary of Events and Information	Remarks and references to Appendices
MAP GERMANY 1/100,000	1918			
	Dec 17	8 pm	D.A.C. moved to MEISNES.	See
	18	8 pm	Resting and cleaning up Harness Equipment, etc.	See
	19	8 pm	Resting and cleaning up Harness Equipment, etc.	See
	20	8 pm	Resting and cleaning up Harness Equipment, etc.	See
	21	8 pm	D.A.C. marched to ELSENBORNE LAGER	See
GERMANY 1/100,000	22	8 pm	D.A.C. marched to KALTER HERBERGER	See
	23	8 pm	D.A.C. marched to HARPERSCHEID.	See
	24	8 pm	Resting and cleaning up Harness Equipment, etc.	See
	25	8 pm	D.A.C. marched t: - HQ and No 1 Echelon to KALL No 2 and 3 Sections to SÖTENICH	See
	26	8 pm	Resting and cleaning up of Harness Equipment, etc.	See
	27	9 am	Lieut. Lee returned from Cour	
	28	8 pm	Lieut. Lee to Woolwich proceeded on Course Ordnance Command Internal reinforcements arrived 25-342 Bde 4 - 310 Bde 5 - DAC 1 - Ordnance from 4th D.A.C. 17. D.K.C. 17. 12. 18 Appear 4 C.G. 19. 20. 12. 18	
	29	8 pm	11 O.R. Demobilised	
	30	8 pm	5 O.R. ditto	
	31	8 pm		

Army Form C. 2118.

62D Aus CCS

ORIGINAL COPY WAR DIARY
or
INTELLIGENCE SUMMARY.
(Erase heading not required.)

JANUARY / 19   Vol No 5

Instructions regarding War Diaries and Intelligence
Summaries are contained in F. S. Regs., Part II.
and the Staff Manual respectively. Title pages
will be prepared in manuscript.

Place	Date	Hour	Summary of Events and Information	Remarks and references to Appendices
	1919			
CALL. GERMANY	Jan 1	8 P.m.	8 Holiday and Recreational Training	
	2	"	ditto	
	3	"	ditto	
	4	"	ditto	
	5	"	ditto	
	6	"	ditto	
	7	"	ditto	
	8	"	ditto	
	9	"	ditto	
	10	"	4 NCO's reinforcements joined 2 to No 1 Section 2 to No 3 Section.	
	11	"	Holiday and Recreational Training	
	12	"	ditto	
	13	"	1 Farrier Sgt joined and posted to No 2 Section. Lieut Owen proceeded on leave	
	14	"	Holiday and Recreational Training	
	15	"	ditto	
	16	"	ditto	

Army Form C. 2118.

WAR DIARY
or
INTELLIGENCE SUMMARY.
(Erase heading not required.)

Instructions regarding War Diaries and Intelligence Summaries are contained in F. S. Regs., Part II. and the Staff Manual respectively. Title pages will be prepared in manuscript.

Place	Date	Hour	Summary of Events and Information	Remarks and references to Appendices
	1919			
	Jan			
	17th	8pm	Military and Recreational Training.	L
	18th	8pm	1 Sgt 2 Corporals M.M.P. attached. Men inspected by Selection Board.	L
	19th	8pm	Military and Recreational Training. Lieut Colonel H.A. Woodcock DSO relieved from Comd and assumed Comd of Column	L
	20th	8pm	d°.	L
	21st	8pm	Lieut Colonel H.A. Woodcock DSO Capt W.H.S. Long No. 70403 Cpl. Crees J awarded Croix de Guerre with Gold Star 20.1.1919 2nd Corp RFA	Jaw
	22	8pm	Military and Recreational Training	Jaw
	23	8pm	d°.	Jaw
	24	8pm	d°.	Jaw
	25	8pm	d°. 2 O.R. proceeded to England for Demobilization	Jaw
	26	8pm	d°. 5 Indian Reinforcements joined. 1 O.R. proceeded on leave to U.K.	Jaw
	27	8pm	d°. 1 Officer 2 O.R. proceeded to England for Demobilization	Jaw
	28	8pm	d°. 5 O.R. d°. d°.	Jaw
	29	8pm	d°. 1 O.R. joined, 2Lieut E.O. Badham Jackson struck off strength.	Jaw
	30	8pm	d°. Capt J Ebersdorf invalided on leave, Capt J Tragen no 78059 Sgt C.H. Taylor rendered non-effective	Jaw
	31	8pm	d°.	Jaw

J. Meredith Lieut Col PSC
Commanding 62(WR) O.C.

SECRET

WAR DIARY
62nd DIVL. ARTY
FEBRUARY 1919

Vol. XIV

Army Form C. 2118.

WAR DIARY
or
INTELLIGENCE SUMMARY.
(Erase heading not required.)

FEBRUARY

Instructions regarding War Diaries and Intelligence Summaries are contained in F. S. Regs., Part II. and the Staff Manual respectively. Title pages will be prepared in manuscript.

Place	Date	Hour	Summary of Events and Information	Remarks and references to Appendices
Cole Germany	1919 Feb 1	8pm	Military and Recreational Training	Nee
	2	8pm	ditto	Nee
	3	8pm	ditto	Nee
	4	8pm	ditto	Nee
	5	8pm	ditto	Nee
	6	8pm	ditto	Nee
	7	8pm	ditto	Nee
	8	8pm	ditto	Nee
	9	8pm	ditto	Nee
	10	8pm	ditto	Nee
	11	8pm	ditto	Nee
	12	8pm	ditto	Nee
	13	8pm	ditto	Nee
	14	8pm	ditto Capt R.H.S. Long proceeded on leave. Sent off much corr agreed duties of Adjutant	Nee
	15	8pm	ditto	Nee
	16	8pm	ditto	Nee

T.2134. Wt. W708—776. 50000. 4/15. Sir J. C. & S.

Army Form C. 2118.

WAR DIARY
or
INTELLIGENCE SUMMARY.
(Erase heading not required.)

FEBRUARY

Place	Date	Hour	Summary of Events and Information	Remarks and references to Appendices
Camp Luneray	1919			
	Feb 17	8 am	Military and Recreational Training	See
	18	8 am	ditto	See
	19	8 am	Inspection by 506 R.A.	See
	20	8 am	ditto	See
	21	8 am	ditto	See
	22	8 am	ditto	See
	23	8 am	Lieut J. Watts assumed duties of Adjutant	See
	24	8 am	ditto	See
	25	8 am	ditto	See
	26	8 am	ditto	See
	27	8 am	ditto	See
	28	8 am	ditto	See

J.A. Cockburn Capt. 16. P. Ser.
Comdg 16.

War Diary

Original

Highland

Divisional Ammunition Column

Volume No. 8 '27 March.

ORIGINAL

Army Form C. 2118.

WAR DIARY
or
INTELLIGENCE SUMMARY.

(Erase heading not required.)

Instructions regarding War Diaries and Intelligence Summaries are contained in F. S. Regs., Part II. and the Staff Manual respectively. Title pages will be prepared in manuscript.

Month: March.

Place	Date	Hour	Summary of Events and Information	Remarks and references to Appendices
CNL GERMANY	1917 Mar 1	8p.m	Military and Recreational Training	two
	2	d.	ditto	three
	3	d.	ditto	three
	4	d.	ditto	three
	5	d.	ditto	three
	6	d.	ditto	three
	7	d.	ditto. 2/Lieut A.H. Maybee joined and posted to No.2. Section	three
	8	d.	ditto	three
	9	d.	ditto	three
	10	d.	ditto. Capt J.S. Edmondson returned from leave	three
	11	d.	ditto	three
	12	d.	ditto	three
	13	d.	d. d.	three
	14	d.	d. d.	three
	15	d.	ditto. Capt L. Fraser proceeded on leave. Lt Fraser L. commanded No 2. Section	three
	16	d.	ditto. 62(nd) S.O.B. became Highland S.O.B.	three

T.1134. Wt. W708—776. 500000. 4/16. Sir J. C. & S.

CONTINUED

WAR DIARY
or
INTELLIGENCE SUMMARY.
(Erase heading not required.)

Army Form C. 2118.

MARCH.

Place	Date	Hour	Summary of Events and Information	Remarks and references to Appendices
CALL GERMANY PT	1919 Mch 17	8 pm	Military and Recreational Training. Corpl V/85 Long returned from leave	
	18	8 pm	ditto	
	19	8 am	Lt A B Meacham proceeded on leave	
	20	8 am	ditto	
	21	8 am	ditto	
	22	8 pm	Lieut-Col. J A Woodcock ADC proceeded on leave. Corpl A B Kerr L/Cp Haws V/87 Morris MCRC USA & Westgate American E. Force	
	23	8 pm	ditto	
	24	8 am	ditto	
	25	8 am	ditto	
	26	8 am	ditto	
	27	8 am	ditto	
	28	8 pm	9/9 Reinforcements arrived and posted 5 to 3rd Bde. 37 to 2/2 Bde 11 to 2/1 Bde	
	29	8 am	ditto do do do 29 to 3rd Bde 10 to 3rd Feb 11 to 2 Bde	
	30	8 am	ditto Lt L E Bowie RAMC attached	
	31	8 am	ditto	

J Woodcock
LIEUT-COLONEL
COMMANDING HIGHLAND D.A.C.

HIGHLAND D.H.C.

ORIGINAL

MAY

Army Form C. 2118.

WAR DIARY
or
INTELLIGENCE SUMMARY.
(Erase heading not required.)

Place	Date	Hour	Summary of Events and Information	Remarks and references to Appendices
CALL.				
GERMANY	MAY 1st	8 PM		
	2	8 PM	6 REINFORCEMENTS arrived & posted to D.A.C.	
	3	8 PM		
	4	8 PM	H OR to ENGLAND FOR DEMOBILIZATION. 9 Reinforcements arrived & posted to D.A.C.	
	5	8 PM	G.O.C. R.A. 2nd ARMY inspected D.A.C.	
	6	8 PM	2/LIEUT. H.C. INKSON proceeded on leave.	
	7	8 PM	D.A.C. marched to :- H Q and No.1 SECTION to BURVENICH. No.2 SECTION to EICKS. No.3 SECTION to GLEHN.	
	8	8 PM	23 N.R. to ENGLAND for DEMOBILIZATION.	
	9	8 PM	1 REINFORCEMENT arrived and posted to 312th BDE.	
	10	8 PM		
	11	8 PM	19 L.D. MULES transferred to 310th BRIGADE. R.F.A.	
	12	8 PM		
	13	8 PM		
	14	8 PM		
	15	8 PM		
	16	8 PM	1 O.R. to ENGLAND for Demobilization	

HIGHLAND DAC

ORIGINAL
MAY

Army Form C. 2118.

WAR DIARY
or
INTELLIGENCE SUMMARY.
(Erase heading not required.)

Instructions regarding War Diaries and Intelligence Summaries are contained in F. S. Regs., Part II. and the Staff Manual respectively. Title pages will be prepared in manuscript.

Place	Date	Hour	Summary of Events and Information	Remarks and references to Appendices
	1919			
BURTERICK	MAY 16	8pm	CAPT. CANDY JOINED AND POSTED TO MOT. SECTION.	
"	17	8pm		
"	18	8pm		
"	19	8pm		
"	20	8pm		
"	21	8pm	Lieut. Col. H.O. Woodcock D.S.O. proceeded on leave. Capt. Candy A/Lt. assumed Command	
	22	8pm		
	23	8pm		
	24	8pm	Lieut. Col. H.O. Woodcock D.S.O. recalled from leave. 1 Officer to L.U.K. to hospital	
	25	8pm		
	26	8pm		
	27	8pm	14 Reinforcements arrived	
	28	8pm		
	29	8pm	G.O.C. Highland Division inspected D.A.C. stables, billets & at Evening.	
	30	8pm		
	31	8pm	3 Reinforcements arrived	

HWoodcock
Lt. Col. 31/5/19
Comm. Highland D.A.C.

Confidential.

WAR DAIRY

of

D.A.C. HIGHLAND Division.

From 1/9/19   To 30/9/19.

ORIGINAL

Army Form C. 2118.

WAR DIARY
or
INTELLIGENCE SUMMARY.
(Erase heading not required.)

HIGHLAND D.A.C.

JUNE 1919.

Instructions regarding War Diaries and Intelligence Summaries are contained in F. S. Regs., Part II. and the Staff Manual respectively. Title pages will be prepared in manuscript.

Place	Date	Hour	Summary of Events and Information	Remarks and references to Appendices
Bordenich Germany	June 1st	8/am	2/Lt J. A. Hooker. R.F.A. Joined & Posted No. 3 Section	
	2nd	"	5 Reinforcements arrived & posted. 3 to H.Qr 2 to S.A.A. Section	
	3rd	"		
	4th	"	Lt.-Col. F. A. Woodcock. D.S.O. proceeded on leave. Capt. A. F. Canoly assumed Command	
	5th	"		
	6th	"		
	7th	"		
	8th	"	Capt. J. E. Edmondson. proceeded on leave.	
	9th	"		
	10th	"		
	11th	"		
	12th	"	C-in-C inspected D.A.C. Drill Order. Lt. H. E. Richards transferred to U.K.	
	13th	"	Capt. L. H. Paton. transferred to U.K.	
	14th	"	1 Reinforcement arrived & posted to No. 2 Section	
	15th	"		
	16th	"		

Army Form C. 2118.

WAR DIARY
or
INTELLIGENCE SUMMARY.
(Erase heading not required.)

Instructions regarding War Diaries and Intelligence Summaries are contained in F. S. Regs., Part II. and the Staff Manual respectively. Title pages will be prepared in manuscript.

Place	Date	Hour	Summary of Events and Information	Remarks and references to Appendices
Bissendorf Germany	June 17th	8 pm	Capt. J. E. Edmondson. Recalled from leave.	
	18th	"	Lt.-Col. J. A. Woodcock. D.S.O. returned from leave & re-assumed Command.	
	19th	"	Lieut. H. A. Bellairs R.F.A. joined & posted to No 1 Section. 1 Reinforcement arrived & posted to S.A.A. Section.	
	19th	"		
	20th	"		
	21st	"	1 O.R. arrived & posted from D/245 Bgde. R.F.A.	
	22nd	"		
	23rd	"	25 Indian Reinforcements arrived & posted. 2 Reinforcements arrived & posted.	
	24th	"	1 O.R. to England for Demobilization.	
	25th	"	12 Reinforcements arrived & posted.	
	26th	"		
	27th	"	Capt. V.H.S. Long proceeded on leave. Lieut. J.B. Wist. assumed duty of A/Adjutant.	
	28th	"	Lieut. H. A. Bellairs transferred to U.K. Peace Terms signed with Germany.	
	29th	"		
	30th	"	5 Reinforcements arrived & posted.	

JWoodcock
Lt. Colonel.
Commanding, Highborne Divl. Amm. Column.

T2134. Wt. W708—776. 500000. 4/15. Sir J. C. & S.

ORIGINAL.

WAR DIARY.

HIGHLAND DIVISIONAL AMMN. COLUMN.

JULY. 1919.

VOLUME No. 7.

ORIGINAL

Army Form C. 2118.

HIGHLAND DIV AMMN COLUMN.

WAR DIARY
or
~~INTELLIGENCE~~ SUMMARY.

(Erase heading not required.)

JULY 1919.

Instructions regarding War Diaries and Intelligence Summaries are contained in F. S. Regs., Part II. and the Staff Manual respectively. Title pages will be prepared in manuscript.

Place	Date	Hour	Summary of Events and Information	Remarks and references to Appendices
Burvenich. Germany	1st	8 pm	Captain A F Candy. proceeded on leave. 1 O.R. arrived and posted.	See
	2nd	"	1 O.R. arrived and posted.	See
	3rd	"	Captain J Fraser proceeded on leave.	See
	4th	"	2 O.R. to England for Demobilization.	See
	5th	"		See
	6th	"		See
	7th	"	Rev W Cooksey (C.F) posted to 37th C.C.S. Rev A Kelleher (C.F) joined and posted.	See
	8th	"	1 O.R. to England for Demobilization. Holiday for Peace Celebrations.	See
	9th	"		See
	10th	"		See
	11th	"	1 O.R. to England for Demobilization.	See
	12th	"		See
	13th	"	Captain V H S Long returned from leave and re-assumed duties of Adjutant.	See
	14th	"		See
	15th	"		See
	16th	"	Captain A F Candy returned from leave.	See

Army Form C. 2118.

WAR DIARY
or
INTELLIGENCE/SUMMARY.
(Erase heading not required.)

JULY 1919

Instructions regarding War Diaries and Intelligence Summaries are contained in F. S. Regs., Part II. and the Staff Manual respectively. Title pages will be prepared in manuscript.

Place	Date	Hour	Summary of Events and Information	Remarks and references to Appendices
Burvenich Germany	17th	3 pm	R.S.M. (W.O.1) joined and posted.	
	18th	"		
	19th	"	D.A.C. Sports.	
	20th	"	1 L.D. Horse & 9 Mules to Animal Collecting Camp DUREN, for Sale.	
	21st	"		
	22nd	"	1 O.R. to England for Demobilization.	
	23rd	"		
	24th	"		
	25th	"		
	26th	"	20 Mules to Animal Collecting Camp. Duren, for Sale. 32 Indian Reinforcements arrived and posted. Captain J Fraser returned from leave.	
	27th	"		
	28th	"		
	29th	"		
	30th	"		
	31st	"		

Goodrick
Lieut-Colonel
Commanding, Highland Div¹ Amm. Column.

ORIGINAL

WAR DIARY

HIGHLAND DIVISIONAL. AMMN. COLUMN

AUGUST 1919

VOLUME N° 8

Army Form C. 2118.

HIGHLAND DIVISIONAL AMMUNITION COLUMN

ORIGINAL

WAR DIARY
or
INTELLIGENCE SUMMARY.   AUGUST 1919.

(Erase heading not required.)

Instructions regarding War Diaries and Intelligence
Summaries are contained in F. S. Regs., Part II.
and the Staff Manual respectively. Title pages
will be prepared in manuscript.

Place	Date	Hour	Summary of Events and Information	Remarks and references to Appendices
CODFORD WILTS.	1st	8pm		
	2nd	"		
	3rd	"		
	4th	"	Captain V H S LONG RFA posted to Eastern Divisional Artillery. Lieut F H HEMPEL RFA assumed duty of Adjutant.	
	5th	"	44 Horses to Remount Depot for England. 1 18pdr Training Gun returned to I.O.M. (from No 2 Section) Workshops DUREN.	
	6th	"	2,000 rounds 18 pdr Ammunition. 2,000 rounds 4.5 How Ammunition. 180,000 rounds S A A returned to Dump at Westhoven. 1 18pdr Training Gun (No 1 Section) and 1 4.5 How (SAA Section) to I.C.S. DUREN.	
	7th	"	Moved 310th Brigade R F A complete to DUREN.	
	8th	"	1 O.R. to England for dispersal. 43 Horses to Remount Depot COLOGNE. All D A C vehicles loaded with G1098 Mob stores, less Harness, to Duren to proceed to U.K.	
	9th	"	428 Mules to Animal Collecting Camp DUREN. 5 Motor Lorries conveyed all D A C harness to DUREN to proceed to U.K.	
	10th	"		
	11th	"		
	12th	"		
	13th	"	D A C Personnel marched to DUREN BARRACKS.	
	14th	"	D A C Personnel entrained at DUREN.	

Army Form C. 2118.

WAR DIARY
or
INTELLIGENCE SUMMARY.

August 1919

(Erase heading not required.)

Instructions regarding War Diaries and Intelligence Summaries are contained in F. S. Regs., Part II. and the Staff Manual respectively. Title pages will be prepared in manuscript.

Place	Date	Hour	Summary of Events and Information	Remarks and references to Appendices
GODFORD Wilts	15th	8pm		Nil
	16th	"	D A C Personnel detrained at CALAIS.	Nil
			D A C Personnel embarked CALAIS and disembarked DOVER.	Nil
			D A C Personnel entrained at DOVER and detrained CODFORD. 119m.	Nil
	17th	"		Nil
	18th	"		Nil
	19th	"		Nil
	20th	"	Captain J E Edmondson R F A proceeded on leave.	Nil
	21st	"	1 O.R. to Concentration Camp for dispersal.	Nil
	22nd	"		Nil
	23rd	"		Nil
	24th	"		Nil
	25th	"		Nil
	26th	"		Nil
	27th	"		Nil
	28th	"	Captain A F Candy R F A proceeded on leave.	Nil
	29th	"		Nil
	30th	"	12 O.R. to Concentration Camp for Dispersal.	Nil
	31st	"		Nil

F Woodcock
Lieut-Colonel R F A
Commanding, Highland Divisional Ammn Column.

www.ingramcontent.com/pod-product-compliance
Lightning Source LLC
Chambersburg PA
CBHW081432160426
43193CB00013B/2262